U0925174

我们总以为生命中有些东西永远不会消失，可它总是在我们意识到之前便转瞬即逝了……这就是青春。而我们要记住的是，幸福只是行进中的旅程，不是目的地。

Something that we used to think would last forever in our lives, had actually vanished in a second before we realized it... This is youth, and we should remember that happiness is a way of travel, not a destination.

青春是华丽的旅行

詹少晶／编译

江苏人民出版社

图书在版编目（CIP）数据

青春是华丽的旅行：英汉对照 / 詹少晶编译．-- 南京：江苏人民出版社，2016.1
ISBN 978-7-214-12871-3

Ⅰ．①青…　Ⅱ．①詹…　Ⅲ．①英语－汉语－对照读物　Ⅳ．① H319.4

中国版本图书馆 CIP 数据核字（2015）第 315170 号

书　　名　青春是华丽的旅行：英汉对照
编 译 者　詹少晶
责任编辑　朱　超
装帧设计　浪殿设计　飞　扬
版式设计　张文艺
出版发行　凤凰出版传媒股份有限公司
　　　　　江苏人民出版社
出版社地址　南京市湖南路1号A楼，邮编：210009
出版社网址　http://www.jspph.com
　　　　　http://jsrmcbs.tmall.com
经　　销　凤凰出版传媒股份有限公司
印　　刷　北京中印联印务有限公司
开　　本　718 毫米 ×1000 毫米 1/16
印　　张　12
字　　数　153 千字
版　　次　2016 年 5 月第 1 版　2016 年 5 月第 1 次印刷
标准书号　978-7-214-12871-3
定　　价　24.00元

Youth Is a Journey Full of Flowers
青春是华丽的旅行

青春的旅途不一定始终是美好的，但是那些挣扎可以让你变得更加坚强，那些改变可以让你变得更有智慧。

前 言 | PREFACE

Youth
青春

◎ Samuel Ullman

Youth is not a time of life; it is a state of mind; it is not a matter of rosy cheeks, red lips and supple knees; it is a matter of the will, a quality of the imagination, a vigor of the emotions; it is the freshness of the deep springs of life. Youth means a tempera-mental predominance of courage over timidity, of the appetite for adventure over the love of ease. This often exists in a man of 60 more than a boy of 20. Nobody grows old merely by a number of years. We grow old by deserting our ideals. Years may wrinkle the skin, but to give up enthusiasm wrinkles the soul. Worry, fear, self-distrust bows the heart and turns the spring back to dust. Whether 60 or 16, there is in every human being's heart the lure of wonder, the unfailing childlike appetite of what's next and the joy of the game of living. In the center of your heart and my heart there is a wireless station: so long as it receives messages of beauty, hope, cheer, courage and power from men and from the Infinite, so long are you young. When the aerials are down, and your spirit is covered with snows of cynicism and the ice of pessimism, then you are grown old, even at 20, but as long as your aerials are up, to catch waves of optimism, there is hope you may die young at 80.

青春不是年华，而是一种心态；青春不是红润的双颊、鲜红的双唇、柔软的双膝，而是坚忍的意志、丰富的想象、炽热的情感；青春是生命之泉在喷涌。青春是气贯长虹的勇气，它能战胜怯弱；青春是勇于冒险的渴望，它打败苟安。这股精神，二十岁的人身上有，但六十岁的人身上更多见。年岁的增加，并非真正的衰老。真正的衰老始于放弃理想的那一刻。悠悠岁月，老去的只是容颜；抛弃激情，衰败的却是灵魂。忧心、恐惧、缺乏自信会使心灵扭曲，意气如灰。不论花甲之年，还是芳龄十六，奇迹的诱惑、生命的欢乐和孩童般的天真都永存心间。你我心中，都有一台天线：只要你从天地间接收美好、希望、快乐、勇气和力量，你便会青春永驻。一旦天线掉下来，这股精神就会被冰雪覆盖，变得玩世不恭。即便你芳龄二十，实则早已老去。然而，只要你竖起天线，接收乐观的信号，即使在八十岁时告别尘世，你仍会觉得年轻。

目 录 | CONTENTS

站在青春的起点

镌刻成长的印记

踏上梦想的舞台

走向最美的旅行

站在青春的起点

Leave the excess baggage of yesterday's mistakes and dare to enter into all the tomorrow. Leave yesterday to history and resolve to begin fresh each new day daring to make dreams become a reality.

放下昨日错误的重负，勇敢融入明日的生活。将昨日留给历史，满怀信心地迎接每个新日子的到来，努力将梦想变为现实。

The Beginning
起点

© Deng M. T.

In the beginning, all things are hopeful. We prepare ourselves to start a new. Though we may be intent on the magnificent journey ahead, all things are contained in the first moment: our optimism, our faith, our resolution, our innocence.

In order to start, we must make a decision. The decision is a commitment to daily self-cultivation. We must make a strong connection to our inner selves. Outside matters are **superfluous**[①]. Alone and naked, we negotiate all of life's travails. Therefore, we alone must make something of ourselves, transforming ourselves into the instruments for experiencing the deepest spiritual essence of life.

Once we make our decision, all things will come to us. **Auspicious**[②] signs are not a superstition, but a confirmation. They are a response. It is said that if one chooses to pray to a rock with enough devotion, even that rock will come alive. In the same way, once we choose to commit ourselves to spiritual practice, even the mountains and valleys will **reverberate**[③] to the sound of our decision.

---

① superfluous [sju'pə:fluəs] adj. 过剩的；多余的，不必要的

② auspicious [ɔ:'spiʃəs] adj. 吉兆的，吉利的；兴盛的，幸运的

③ reverberate [ri'və:bəreit] v.（使）回响，（使）反射

美丽语录

It's time to start living the life you've imagined.

是时候开始过自己想要的生活了。

在起点，所有的一切都充满希望。我们准备重新开始。虽然我们的目的是前方奇妙的旅程，但我们的一切希望——乐观、信念、决心和纯真，却都包含在开始的那一刻。

为了开始，我们必须作好决定。这一决定是我们日常自我修养的一种承诺。我们要将它与自己的内心建立一种密切的关联。除此之外的事都是多余的。我们终生劳碌，最终孤独而赤裸地离去。因此，我们必须有所作为，那样可以引导我们去体会生活中最深层的精神实质。

一旦我们下定决心，所有的事情就会接连不断地发生。吉兆并非迷信，而是对事情的肯定预测，是事物的反应。据说，若有人虔诚地向岩石祈祷，岩石都会被赋予生命。同样，若我们坚定自己的精神之旅，即使高山和峡谷也会回应我们坚定的呼声。

年轻人

◎ Aristotle

To begin with the Youthful type of character. Young men have strong passions, and tend to gratify them **indiscriminately**①. They are changeable and fickle in their desires, which are violent while they last, but quickly over: their impulses are keen but not deep-rooted, and are like sick people's attacks of hunger and thirst. They are hot-tempered, and quick-tempered, and apt to give way to their anger; bad temper often gets the better of them, for owing to their love of honour they cannot bear being slighted, and are indignant if they imagine themselves unfairly treated. While they love honour, they love victory still more; for youth is eager for superiority over others, and victory is one form of this. They love both more than they love money, which indeed they love very little, not having yet learnt what it means to be without it—this is the point of Pittancus, remark about Amphiaraus. They look at the good side rather than the bad, not having yet witnessed many instances of wickedness. They trust others readily, because they have not yet often been cheated.

They are **sanguine**②; nature warms their blood as though with excess of wine; and besides that, they have as yet met with few disappointments. Their

① indiscriminately [indi'skrimənitli] adv. 不加选择地；随意地

② sanguine ['sæŋgwin] adj. 乐观的；血色好的，红润的

美丽语录

One day I passed, one day I missed...one day left, I gotta grasp it.

一天路过，一天错过……还有一天，好好把握。

首先讨论一下年轻人的性格特征。年轻人激情似火，而且经常不加思索就予以满足。他们的愿望变化莫测、反覆无常，来时强烈无比，去时转瞬即逝。他们极易冲动，但并非根深蒂固，就像病人遭到饥渴的侵袭一样。他们热情似火、性情暴躁，常常管不住自己的脾气。他们珍惜荣誉，他们无法忍受被人忽视，因此，一旦发现自己遭遇不公平的对待，便会义愤填膺。他们珍惜荣誉，但他们更爱胜利。因为年轻人总喜欢胜人一筹，而胜利就是一种绝好的表现方式。他们钟爱荣誉和胜利要多过金钱，他们之所以不在意金钱，是因为他们还未明白缺少金钱意味着什么——庇塔喀斯就是这样评论安菲阿劳斯的。他们未曾亲眼目睹过多少邪恶之事，所以他们总是看到事物好的一面，而非不好的那一面。他们全心全意相信别人，只因为他们很少上当受骗。

他们面色红润，大自然好像用了过多的葡萄酒来温暖他们的血液；除此之外，他们没有遇过多少挫折。他们总是在期盼中度日，而不是在回忆

lives are mainly spent not in memory but in expectation; for expectation refers to the future, memory to the past, and youth has a long future before it and a short past behind it: on the first day of one's life one has nothing at all to remember, and can only look forward.

They are easily cheated, owing to the sanguine disposition just mentioned. Their hot tempers and hopeful dispositions make them more courageous than older men are; the hot temper prevents fear, and the hopeful disposition creates confidence; we cannot feel tear so long as we are feeling angry, and any expectation of good makes us confident.

They are shy, accepting the rules of society in which they have been trained, and not yet believing in any other standard of honor. They have exalted notions, because they have not yet been humbled by life or learnt its necessary limitations; moreover, their hopeful disposition makes them think themselves equal to great things and that means having exalted notions. They would always rather do noble deeds than useful ones: their lives are regulated more by moral feeling than by reasoning; and whereas reasoning leads us to choose what is useful, moral goodness leads us to choose what is noble.

They are fonder of their friends, intimates, and companions than older men are, because they like spending their days in the company of others, and have not yet come to value either their friends or anything else by their usefulness to themselves. All their mistakes are in the direction of doing things excessively and **vehemently**[①]. They disobey Chilon's precept by overdoing everything, they love too much and hate too much, and the same thing with everything else. They think they know everything, and are always quite sure about it; this, in fact, is

① vehemently ['vi:iməntli] adv. 激烈地，强烈地；热切地

中缅怀；因为期盼意味着未来，而回忆意味着过去。未来还有很长的日子等着年轻人，过去的岁月只是微小的一部分。一个人来到世上的第一天，他没有什么能回忆的事情，他能做的只有期盼未来。

他们容易上当受骗，只因上面提到的精力旺盛的脾性。火一般的热情、满怀希望的天性让他们比老年人更有胆量。如火的热情让他们不知恐惧，希望的天性让他们自信满满。我们感到愤怒的时候，便全然不知泪水，而对美好事物的憧憬又让我们充满自信。

他们是害羞的，顺其自然地遵守社会惯例，却不相信任何荣誉标准。他们有着崇高的理想，因为生活还未教会他们如何谦卑，如何理解那些必要的束缚。再者，他们满怀希望的天性，让他们以为自己和日月无异——这就是他们所谓的崇高理想。他们宁可做一些高尚之事，也不做有用之事。他们的生活多由道德感观操控，而非理智。尽管理智指引我们去做有用之事，而道德品质则指引我们去做高尚之事。

和老年人相比，他们更喜欢自己的朋友、密友和伙伴，因为有人相伴的日子才是他们的最爱，而且不论是朋友或是其他东西，都不以其实用性作为价值的判断标准。他们所犯的错，都是因为做事过度或者过猛。他们不遵守齐隆法则，凡事做得太过头，他们不是爱得太深，就是恨得太多，做其他事也是如此。他们总觉得自己无所不知，而且自信满满。实际上，

why they overdo everything... They are ready to pity others, because they think everyone an honest man, or anyhow better than he is: they judge their neighbor by their own harmless natures, and so cannot think he deserves to be treated in that way. They are fond of fun and therefore witty, wit being well-bred insolence.

这就是他们行事过头的症结所在……他们随时准备着同情别人，因为他们觉得每个人都是诚实的，或者要比自己的为人好——他们用自己的善良本性来判断邻里，总觉得自己不该得到这样的对待。他们喜欢玩乐，因而非常机智幽默——这就是一种低调的傲慢。

A Lesson of Life
生活的一课

© Ronald Reagan

"Everything happens for the best." my mother said whenever I faced disappointment. "If you can carry on, one day something good will happen. And you'll realize that it wouldn't have happened if not for that previous disappointment."

Mother was right, as I discovered after graduating from college in 1932. I had decided to try for a job in radio, then work my way up to sports announcer. I **hitchhiked**[①] to Chicago and knocked on the door of every station—and got turned down every time.

In one studio, a kind lady told me that big stations couldn't risk hiring inexperienced person—"Go out in the sticks and find a small station that'll give you a chance." she said.

I thumbed home to Dixon, Illinois. While there was no radio-announcing jobs in Dixon, my father said Montgomery Ward had opened a store and wanted a local athlete to manage its sports department. Since Dixon was where I had played high school football, I applied. The job sounded just right for me. But I

① hitchhike [ˈhitʃˌhaik] v. 搭便车（旅行）

美丽语录

When your day has been like a hurricane, all you can do is looking forward to the rainbow that follows.

如果你的生活经历了一场暴风雨，你要做的就是期待雨后的那缕彩虹。

每当我遇到挫折时，母亲就会说："一切都会好的。只要你坚持下去，总有一天会有好事发生。你会认识到，如果没有以前的挫折，就不会有现在的一切。"

母亲是对的，我是在 1932 年大学刚毕业的时候发现了这一点。我已决定试着在电台找个事儿做，然后争取做体育节目的播音员。我搭便车到了芝加哥，挨个敲电台的门推销自己——但每次都被拒绝了。

在一个播音室里，一位好心的女士告诉我，大的广播电台是不会冒险雇用没经验的新手的——"去乡下找一家给你机会的小电台吧。"她说。

我搭车来到我的家乡，那是伊利诺斯州的迪克森。在迪克森当时还没有电台播音员这样的工作，父亲说，蒙哥马利·沃德开了一家新商店，想雇请一个本地的运动员管理店里的体育部。我中学时曾在迪克森打过橄榄球，所以我去申请了这份工作。工作听起来挺适合我的，但是我没被聘用。

wasn't hired.

My disappointment must have shown. "Everything happens for the best." Mom reminded me. Dad offered me the car to job hunt. I tried WOC Radio in Davenport, Iowa. The program director, a wonderful Scotsman named Peter MacArthur, told me they had already hired an announcer.

As I left his office, my **frustration**[1] boiled over. I asked aloud, "How can a fellow get to be a sport announcer if he can't get a job in a radio station?"

I was waiting for the elevator when I heard MacArthur calling, "What was that you said about sports? Do you know anything about football?" Then he stood me before a microphone and asked me to broadcast an imaginary game.

On my way home, as I have many times since, I thought of my mother's words: "If you carry on, one day something good will happen. Something wouldn't have happened if not for that previous disappointment." I often wonder what direction my life might have taken if I'd gotten the job at Montgomery Ward.

① frustration [frʌs'treiʃən] n. 挫折，失败，挫败

我的沮丧心情一定表现出来了。“一切总会好的。”母亲提醒我说。爸爸给了我一辆汽车找工作用。我试着到爱荷华州达文波特的 WOC 电台去求职。那里的电台节目总监是一个很棒的苏格兰人，名叫彼得·麦克阿瑟，他告诉我他们已经雇到播音员了。

离开他的办公室时，我的挫折感达到了极点。我大声地说："一个连在电台都找不到工作的家伙又怎么能成为体育节目的播音员呢？"

等电梯时，我听到麦克阿瑟喊道："你说什么体育？你懂橄榄球吗？"接着他让我站到麦克风前面，请我解说一场想象中的比赛。

在回家的路上——以后也有很多次，我思考着母亲的那句话："只要你坚持下去，总要一天会有好事发生。如果没有以前的挫折，就不会有现在的一切。"我常想，如果当年我得到蒙哥马利·沃德的那份工作，我的人生之路又会怎样走呢？

Thinking Is the Premise of Success

思考是成功的前提

◎ Harv Eker

Thinking is necessary if you want to succeed in life. People fear that thinking may upset their comfort and self-satisfaction. Thinking needs constant practice with enthusiasm, enthusiasm generates interest and sustains thinking. And concentration will help us form a clear picture in our minds of the ultimate objective.

Thinking should be constant and continuous. With concentration, we can arrange thoughts in order and become a rapid thinker. It is also important to develop organized thinking learning to think of different things one by one in order. We can **stimulate**[①] thinking power by taking part in serious conversations or discussion and defending our positions so that it will drive us to think more clearly and objectively. Reading books and magazines will also help us in the process of formulating ideas.

Positive thinking has a **tremendous**[②] influence over others with whom we come into contact; people who succeed improving their thinking power enrich themselves.

① stimulate ['stimjuleit] v. 刺激，促使，使兴奋

② tremendous [tri'mendəs] adj. 巨大的，惊人的，极度的

美丽语录

If you do not learn to think when you are young, you may never learn.

如果你年轻时不学会思考，那就可能永远不会。

如果你想获得人生的成功，思考是必要的。人们害怕思考会扰乱自己的安逸和自我满足感。思考需要在热情中持续进行，而热情会激发人的兴趣，使思考维持下去。专心致志将有助于我们在脑海中形成有关终极目标的清晰画面。

思考应该是持续不断的。如果集中精力，我们就能理清思绪，成为反应敏捷的思想者。培养清晰有条理的思考习惯，学会依次考虑不同的事情，这也同样重要。我们可以通过参加认真严谨的谈话或讨论来提高思考能力，也可以进行辩论，这将会促使我们进行更清晰、更客观地思考。阅读书籍和杂志也有助于我们思维的构建。

积极主动的思考对我们接触到的其他人具有巨大的影响力。那些成功提高思考能力的人会充实自己，丰富自己的人生。

To Love Oneself Is the Beginning
爱自己是一场毕生浪漫的开始

◎ Oscar Wilde

To love oneself is the beginning of a lifelong romance.

Love yourself. Love the things that make you you. Your values and talents and memories. Your clothes, your nose, your **woes**[①]. If you love yourself, you can jump into your life from a springboard of self-confidence. If you love yourself, you can say what you want to say, go where you want to go. The world can be a tough place, and some of the billions of people out there will try to knock you down. Don't join them.

Do things that make you proud, then take pride in what you do. And in who you are.

Who are you anyway? What makes you you? How are you like your **siblings**[②] and neighbors and friends? How are you different? If you were your own secret admirer, what would you most admire?

"My great mistake, the fault for which I can't forgive myself," Oscar Wilde wrote, "is that one day I ceased my **obstinate**[③] pursuit of my own individuality." Keep pursuing your individuality. Keep being yourself. Becoming yourself. It

① woe [wəu] n. 悲痛，灾难，不幸

② sibling ['sibliŋ] n. 兄弟姐妹

③ obstinate ['ɔbstinit] adj. 固执的，顽固的，顽强的

美丽语录

Best case scenario: I love myself; I enjoy living; I smile because I'm happy not because I have to.

最好的情景：爱自己；享受生活；发自内心地微笑。

爱自己是一场毕生浪漫的开始。

爱自己。热爱一切让你成为你自己的事物。你的价值，你的才能，你的回忆。你的衣服，你的鼻子，你的悲伤。如果你爱自己，你就能在自信的跳板上跃入生活。如果你爱自己，你就能畅所欲言，所向披靡。这个世界是冷酷无情的，成千上亿的人等着将你打倒。不要和他们同流合污。

做能让你自豪的事，然后为你所做的事自豪，为自己自豪。

那么，你究竟是谁呢？是什么让你成为你自己呢？你和你的兄弟姐妹、邻居好友又有什么相同点？你有什么与众不同的地方？如果你是自己的秘密崇拜者，那么你最崇拜自己的又是哪一点呢？

“我犯了一个大错，因此我无法原谅我自己，”奥斯卡·王尔德写道，“就是有一天我停止追求自己的个性。”继续追求你的个性。继续做你自己。成为你自己。穿衣和举止与别人一样是件容易的事情。但是，更值得骄傲的事是：让自己与众不同，让自己特别，让自己成为你自己。世界之大，

can be comforting to dress and act like everyone else. But it is grander to be different, to be unique, to be you. I'm the only me in the whole wide world.

There is always one true inner voice. Trust it.

— Gloria Steinem

Sometimes it's hard to know who you are and what you want and whom you like and why you like that person. The answers change because you're changing. Growing. But deep inside, you are you. You were you as a baby, you were you as a kid, and you are you right now. "Let me listen to me and not to them." wrote Gertrude Stein.

It makes sense to consider the advice and opinions of other people. But don't let their noise drown out your inner voice. And don't let the way you sometimes talk or behave in front of others make you lose sight of who you are when you are alone, when you are most you.

"You can live a lifetime and, at the end of it, know more about other people than you know about yourself," aviator Beryl Markham cautioned. Get acquainted with yourself.Tune in to the dreams you have by day and by night. Blend in when you choose to, but appreciate what sets you apart. "The more I like me, the less I want to pretend to be other people." said Jamie Lee Curtis.

唯我是我。

总有一个来自内心的真实之声。听从它吧！

——葛萝莉亚·史丹能

有时，你很难弄清你是谁，你想做什么，你喜欢谁，你又为什么喜欢这个人。你在变，在成长，所以答案也在变。然而，在你内心深处，总有一个声音告诉你：你就是你。不论婴儿还是孩童，你就是现在的你。“让我听从自己的，而不是他们的意见。”葛楚德·史坦写道。

你可以参考别人的意见和看法。但是别让他们的想法淹没你内心的声音。不要因为偶尔出现在人前的谈吐、举止，而忘记独处时的你，那才是最真的自己。

“人活一世，不要临了时才发现，你了解别人要胜过了解自己。”飞行员贝丽尔·马卡姆劝诫道。认识自己。走入你的梦境，不论白天还是黑夜。当你选择走入人群时，那就去做吧！但是，别忘了感谢那些让你与众不同的东西。“我越发爱自己，我就越发不会把自己伪装成别人。”杰米·李·柯蒂斯说道。

Man' Youth
青春物语

◎ Thomas Wolfe

Man's youth is a wonderful thing: it is so full of **anguish**① and of magic and he never comes to know it is, until it has gone from him forever. It is the thing he can't bear to lose, it is the thing whose passing he watches with infinite sorrow and regret, it is the thing whose loss he must lament forever, and it is the thing whose loss he really welcomes with a sad and secret joy, the thing he would never willingly relive again, if it could be restored to him by any magic.

Why is this? The reason is that the strange and bitter miracle of life is nowhere else so evident as in our youth. And what is the essence of that strange and bitter miracle of life which we feel so **poignantly**②, so unutterably, with such a bitter pain and joy, when we are young? It is this: that being rich, we are so poor; that being mighty, we can yet have nothing; that seeing, breathing, smelling, tasting all around us the wealth and glory of this earth, feeling with an intolerable certitude that the whole structure of the enchanted life—the most fortunate, wealthy, good, and happy life that any man has ever known—is ours—

① anguish ['æŋgwiʃ] n. 极度的痛苦；苦恼

② poignantly ['pɔignəntli] adv. 令人辛酸地；强烈地；尖刻地

美丽语录

After all your pains and tears, look at the rainbow of your life. It's totally worth it.

所有的伤痛、眼泪过后，看看生命中的彩虹，一切的一切都是那么的值得。

人的青春奇妙无穷，充满痛楚，充满魔力。青春年少时不知青春为何物，无奈青春一去不复返时才恍然醒悟：青春是谁也不愿失去的东西；眼睁睁看着青春流逝，无限的感伤和遗憾涌上心头；青春的流逝是人们心中永远的痛；青春的流逝让人们或大悲或窃喜；即便魔力可以还以青春，人们也不愿再次经历那些流逝的青春岁月。

为何如此呢？因为青春时代的生活充满了奇特的、心酸的、不平凡的事。青春年少的我们怀着或悲或喜的心情，强烈而又不可名状地体味着那些生活的奇特辛酸史时，我们可曾想过它的本质？它的本质就是：我们富足殷实，却无比贫穷；我们力大无穷，却一无所有；世间的富贵荣华比比皆是，看到，闻到，尝到，甚至可以呼吸到。那份坚信再也无法隐藏了，真真切切感受到整个生活都已陶醉……只要我们向前迈步，努力奋斗，那么人类所知道的最幸运、最富有、最美好、最幸福的生活便立刻属于我们

is ours at once, immediately and forever, the moment that we choose to take a step, or stretch a hand—we yet know that we can really keep, hold, take, and possess forever—nothing. All passes; nothing lasts: the moment that we put our hand upon it, it melts away like smoke, is gone forever, and the snake is eating at our heart again; we see then what we are and what our lives must come to.

A young man is so strong, so mad, so certain, and so lost. He has everything and he is able to use nothing. He hurls the great shoulder of his strength forever against **phantasmal**[①] barriers, he is a wave whose power explodes in lost mid-oceans under timeless skies, he reaches out to grip a fume of painted smoke; he wants all, feels the thirst and power for everything, and finally gets nothing. In the end, he is destroyed by his own strength, devoured by his own hunger, impoverished by his own wealth. Thoughtless of money or the accumulation of material possessions, he is none the less defeated in the end by his own greed.

And that is the reason why, when youth is gone, every man will look back upon that period of his life with infinite sorrow and regret. It is the bitter sorrow and regret of a man who knows that once he had a great talent and wasted it, of a man who knows that once he had a great treasure and got nothing from it, of a man who knows that he had strength enough for everything and never used it.

① phantasmal [fæn'tæzməl] adj. 幻影的；幽灵的；空想的

了，而且将永远属于我们，虽然我们知道，其实我们留不住、抓不着、拿不走也无法占有什么。一切就如过眼云烟，转瞬即逝。我们一伸手，它便像云烟般消失不见了。于是，痛苦再一次啃噬我们的心，我们看到了自己的真面目，明白了未来的生活将何去何从。

青年人非常强壮、狂热、自信，却很容易迷失茫然；他拥有一切，却又无法把握；他身强体壮，想要冲破虚幻的障碍，却像海浪般无力地消失在无边无际的大海中央；他伸出双手想要抓住色彩斑斓的云烟，他想得到一切，渴望主宰一切，可到头来依旧两手空空，一无所获；最后，他被自己的力量打败，被自己的饥饿吞噬，因自己的财富而穷困。他对金钱和财富的积累不以为意，最终必将因为贪念而毁。

这就是为什么当青春消逝，回首过往时，每个人的心中总会充满无限的忧伤和遗憾。曾经杰出的才能，却白白浪费了；曾经殷实的财富，却被挥霍一空；曾经满身的本领，却未好好利用——一个明白了这些道理的人，回忆起青春时代，总会充满忧伤和懊悔。

I Will Persist Until I Succeed

坚持不懈，勇往直前

◎ Og Mandino

In the Orient young bulls are tested for the fight arena in a certain manner. Each is brought to the ring and allowed to attack a **picador**① who pricks them with a lance. The bravery of each bull is then rated with care according to the number of times he demonstrates his willingness to charge in spite of the sting of the blade. Henceforth will I recognize that each day I am tested by life in like manner. If I persist, if I continue to try, if I continue to charge forward, I will succeed.

I was not delivered unto this world in defeat, nor does failure course in my veins. I am not a sheep waiting to be prodded by my shepherd. I am a lion and I refuse to talk, to walk, to sleep with the sheep. I will hear not those who weep and complain, for their disease is contagious. Let them join the sheep. The slaughterhouse of failure is not my destiny.

The prizes of life are at the end of each journey, not near the beginning; and it is not given to me to know how many steps are necessary in order to reach my goal. Failure I may still encounter at the thousandth step, yet success hides

① picador [ˈpikədɔː] n. 骑马斗牛士

美丽语录

Millions of failures are caused by people who do things not thoroughly. It happens that some people cease or give up when it is just one step before success.

世界上千万人的失败，都是失败在做事不彻底，往往做到离成功尚差一步就终止不做了。

在古老的东方，挑选小公牛竞技场格斗有一定的程序。它们被带进场地，向手持长矛的斗牛士攻击。裁判以它受激后再向斗牛士进攻的次数多少，来评定这只公牛的英勇程度。从今往后，我必须承认，我生命的每一天都在接受这样的考验。如果我坚持不懈，如果我不断尝试，如果我勇往直前，我就一定会成功。

我不是为了失败才来到这个世界上的，我的血管里也没有失败的血液流动。我不是任人驱赶的羔羊。我是猛狮，拒绝与羊群为伍。我不想听失意者的哭泣、抱怨，他们是羊群中的瘟疫。我不能被它传染。失败者的屠宰场不是我命运的归宿。

生命的奖赏远在旅途的终点，而非起点附近。我不知道要走多少步才能达到目标。踏上第一千步的时候，仍可能失败，但成功就隐藏在下一个拐角处，除非我转过拐角，否则永远不知道它是如此接近。

再前进一步。如果没有用，就再向前一步。事实上，每次进步一点点

behind the next bend in the road. Never will I know how close it lies unless I turn the corner.

Always will I take another step. If that is of no avail I will take another, and yet another. In truth, one step at a time is not too difficult.

Henceforth, I will consider each day's effort as but one blow of my blade against a mighty oak. The first blow may cause not a tremor in the wood, nor the second, nor the third. Each blow, of itself, may be trifling, and seem of no consequence. Yet from childish swipes the oak will eventually tumble. So it will be with my efforts of today.

I will be likening to the raindrop which washes away the mountain; the ant who devours a tiger; the star which brightens the earth; the slave who builds a pyramid. I will build my castle one brick at a time for I know that small attempts, repeated, will complete any undertaking.

I will never consider defeat and I will remove from my vocabulary such words and phrases as quit, cannot, unable, impossible, out of the question, improbable, failure, unworkable, hopeless, and retreat; for they are the words of fools. I will avoid despair but if this disease of the mind should infect me then I will work on in despair. I will toil and I will endure. I will ignore the obstacles at my feet and keep my eyes on the goals above my head, for I know that where dry desert ends, green grass grows.

I will remember the ancient law of averages and I will bend it to my good. I will persist with knowledge that each failure to sell will increase my chance for success at the next attempt. Each nay I hear will bring me closer to the sound of yea. Each frown I meet only prepares me for the smile to come. Each misfortune I encounter will carry in it the seed of tomorrow's good luck. I must have the

并不太难。

今后，我承认每一天的努力就像对参天大树的一次砍击。头几刀可能在树林里了无痕迹。每一击本身看似都是微不足道的，似乎毫无结果。然而，累积起来，巨树终会倒下。这恰如我今天的努力。

就像冲洗高山的雨滴，吞噬猛虎的蚂蚁，照亮大地的星辰，建起金字塔的奴隶，我也要一砖一瓦地建造起自己的城堡，因为我深知水滴石穿的道理，只要持之以恒，什么事都可以做到。

我绝不考虑失败，我的字典里不再有放弃、不可能、办不到、没法子、成问题、不大可能、失败，行不通、没希望、退缩……这类愚蠢的字眼。我要尽量避免绝望这种疾病，一旦受到它的威胁，我会立刻设法向它挑战。我要辛勤耕耘，忍受苦楚。我放眼未来，勇往直前，不再理会脚下的障碍。我坚信，沙漠尽头必是绿洲。

我要记住古老的平衡法则，并将其作为我的行为准则。我会牢记每一次的失败都会增加下一次成功的机会。这一次的拒绝就是下一次的赞同，这一次的皱眉就是下一次的笑容。我遭遇的每一个不幸，都预示着明天的好运。夜幕降临，回想一天的遭遇，我总是心存感激。我深知，只有失败多次，才能成功。

night to appreciate the day. I must fail often to succeed only once.

I will try, and try, and try again. Each **obstacle**① I will consider as a mere detour to my goal and a challenge to my profession. I will persist and develop my skills as the mariner develops his, by learning to ride out the wrath of each storm.

Henceforth, I will learn and apply another secret of those who excel in my work. When each day is ended, not regarding whether it has been a success or a failure, I will attempt to achieve one more sale. When my thoughts beckon my tired body homeward I will resist the temptation to depart. I will try again. I will make one more attempt to close with victory, and if that fails I will make another. Never will I allow any day to end with a failure. Thus will I plant the seed of tomorrow's success and gain an **insurmountable**② advantage over those who cease their labor at a prescribed time. When others cease their struggle, the mine will begin, and my harvest will be full.

Nor will I allow yesterday's success to lull me into today's complacency, for this is the great foundation of failure. I will forget the happenings of the day that is gone, whether they were good or bad, and greet the new sun with confidence that this will be the best day of my life.

So long as there is breath in me, that long will I persist. For now I know one of the greatest principles of success; if I persist long enough I will win.

I will persist. I will win.

① obstacle ['ɔbstəkl] n. 障碍（物）；妨碍

② insurmountable [,insə'mauntəbl] adj. 不能克服的；不能超越的

我要尝试，尝试，再尝试。每一个障碍都是我成功之路上的弯道，是对我的挑战。我会坚持和提升自己的能力，像水手一样乘风破浪，渡过每一次暴风雨。

今后，我要学习和借鉴别人成功的秘诀。当每一天结束时，不论是非成败，我全不计较，只坚信明天会更好。当我精疲力竭时，我要抵制回家的诱惑，再试一次。我一试再试。我不会允许任何一天以失败收场。我要为明天的成功播种，超过那些按部就班的人。在别人停滞不前时，我会继续拼搏，终有一天我会丰收。

我不因昨日的成功而自满，因为这是失败的先兆。我要忘却昨日的一切，无论是好是坏，都让它随风而去。我信心百倍，迎接新的太阳，相信今天是我生命中最好的一天。

只要我一息尚存，就要坚持到底。现在我已深知成功的秘诀。如果我坚持不懈，我就有足够的时间赢得胜利。

坚持不懈，终会成功。

The Mirror

镜子的人生哲理

◎ Robert Fulghum

"Dr. Papaderos, what is the meaning of life?"

The usual laughter followed, and people stirred to go.

Papaderos held up his hand and stilled the room and looked at me for a long time, asking with his eyes if I was serious and seeing from my eyes that I was.

"I will answer your question."

Taking his wallet out of his hip pocket, he fished into a leather **billfold**① and brought out a very small round mirror, about the size of a quarter.

And what he said went like this:

"When I was a small child, during the war, we were very poor and we lived in a remote village. One day, on the road, I found the broken pieces of a mirror. A German motorcycle had been wrecked in that place.

"I tried to find all the pieces and put them together, but it was not possible, so I kept only the largest, and, by scratching it on a stone, I made it round. I began to play with it as a toy and became fascinated by the fact that I could reflect light into dark places where the sun would never shine—in deep holes

① billfold ['bilfəuld] n. 皮夹子

美丽语录

You've got a smile that could light up this whole world.

你有一种笑容，可以照亮整个世界。

“帕帕德罗斯博士，生命的价值是什么？”

嘲笑者们又像往常一样笑了起来，人们喧闹着要走。

帕帕德罗斯举起手，示意教室里的人安静。然后，他久久地凝视着我，似乎在审查我是不是认真的。从我的眼神中，他看出我并不是在开玩笑。

“我会回答你的问题。”

他从裤子后面的口袋里掏出皮夹子，从里面拿出一块小圆镜，大小与一个 2 角 5 分的硬币差不多。

而后，他这样说道：

“在战争时期，我还是个小男孩，那时家里很穷，我们住在一个偏僻的小村庄里。有一天，我在马路上发现了许多镜子碎片。曾有一辆德国摩托车在那里发生了事故。

“我试着找到所有的碎片，把它们拼起来，但这是不可能做到的，所以我只留下了那块最大的碎片。在石头上打磨成圆形以后就成了这个样子。我开始拿着它当玩具，发现自己能用它把光线反射到黑暗的地方：深洞、裂缝、漆黑的壁橱等太阳无法照亮的地方。所以，我非常喜欢它，把它当

and crevices and dark closets. It became a game for me to get light into the most inaccessible places I could find.

"I kept the little mirror, and, as I went about nay growing up, I would take it out in idle moments and continue the challenge of the game. As I became a man, I grew to understand that this was not just a child's game but a metaphor for what I might do with my life. I came to understand that I am not the light or the source of light. But light—truth, understanding, knowledge—is there, and it will shine in many dark places only if I reflect it.

"I am a **fragment**① of a mirror whose whole design and shape I do not know. Nevertheless, with what I have I can reflect light into the dark places of this world—into the black places in the hearts of men—and change some things in some people. Perhaps others may see and do likewise. This is what I am about. This is the meaning of my life."

① fragment ['frægmənt] n. 碎片，破片；断片

成一种游戏——让光线进入我能找到的最隐蔽的地方。

“这块小镜子我至今仍保留着，并且，随着自己慢慢地成长，空闲的时候，我还会把它拿出来，继续这种富于挑战的游戏。等我长大成人后，便逐渐明白了，这不仅是一个孩子的游戏，更暗示着我的人生价值。我开始知道自己不是光芒，也不能发出光芒。但是真理、理解和知识这些光芒就在那里，它会照亮许多黑暗的地方，只要我去反射的话。

“我是一面镜子的一块碎片，尽管整个镜子的式样和形状我并不知道。但是，我竭尽所能地反射光芒，照亮世界上那些黑暗的地方——照亮人们心灵的黑暗处——让一些人有所改变。也许有人看到后也会跟我做同样的事。这就是我，这就是我的人生价值。”

Growth That Starts from Thinking
在思考中成长

◎ Eleanor Roosevelt

It seems to me a very difficult thing to put into words the beliefs we hold and what they make you do in your life. I think I was fortunate because I grew up in a family where there was a very deep religious feeling. I don't think it was spoken of a great deal. It was more or less taken for granted that everybody held certain beliefs and needed certain **reinforcements**① of their own strength and that came through your belief in God and your knowledge of prayer.

But as I grew older I questioned a great many of the things that I knew very well my grandmother who had brought me up had taken for granted. And I think I might have been quite a difficult person to live with if it hadn't been for the fact that my husband once said it didn't do you any harm to learn those things, so why not let your children learn them? When they grow up they'll think things out for themselves.

And that gave me a feeling that perhaps that's what we all must do—think out for ourselves what we could believe and how we could live by it. And so I came to the conclusion that you had to use this life to develop the very best that

① reinforcement [ˌriːin'fɔːsmənt] n. 加固，强化；加固物

美丽语录

Just keep your mind open and suck in the experience and if it hurts, it's probably worth it.

只要你敞开心扉去迎接新的经历，哪怕有所疼痛都是值得的！

对我来说，用言语表达我的信仰以及它在我的人生中起到什么作用是一件很难的事情。我想我是幸运的，因为自己成长在一个笃信宗教的家庭里。可我并不觉得家人在时常谈论宗教。每个人心中都有某种信仰，都希望通过自己的力量将其实现，而这种力量就来自对上帝的信仰和懂得如何祈祷。

然而，随着年龄的增长，在祖母身边长大的我也开始质疑那些在她眼中理所应当的东西。我甚至将这些东西拒之门外，仿佛自己成了一个很难相处的人。直到有一次，我的丈夫劝我，这些东西你也学过，对你并无害处，为什么不让孩子们接触呢？他们长大后会懂得如何独立思考这些问题。

丈夫的一番话让我觉得，或许我们每个人都应该这么做——独立思考自己的信仰以及如何在生活中坚守这些信仰。于是，我意识到，人的一生就应该尽力让自己做到最好。

you could develop.

I don't know whether I believe in a future life. I believe that all that you go through here must have some value, therefore there must be some reason. And there must be some "going on". How exactly that happens I've never been able to decide. There is a future—that I'm sure of. But how, that I don't know. And I came to feel that it didn't really matter very much because whatever the future held you'd have to face it when you came to it, just as whatever life holds you have to face it in exactly the same way. And the important thing was that you never let down doing the best that you were able to do—it might be poor because you might not have very much within you to give, or to help other people with, or to live your life with. But as long as you did the very best that you were able to do, then that was what you were put here to do and that was what you were accomplishing by being here.

And so I have tried to follow that out—and not to worry about the future or what was going to happen. I think I am pretty much of a **fatalist**①. You have to accept whatever comes and the only important thing is that you meet it with courage and with the best that you have to give.

① fatalist ['feitəlist] n. 宿命论者

我不知道自己是否相信未来。我相信的是，你所经历的一切都是有价值的，因此也必定是有道理的，必定预示着某些事情即将到来。至于这些事情是如何发生的，我无法决定。但我深信，一定会有未来。至于未来会如何来临，我无从所知。可我开始觉得这一点并不重要，因为无论未来如何，我们都要面对。那么真正重要的是——倾尽全力做到最好。也许你能力有限，帮不上什么大忙，或者无法让自己的生活精彩。但是，只要你倾尽全力，完成自己来到世上的使命，那你就不枉此生了。

我就是这样听从自己的信仰，不再担心未来，不再为即将发生的事情忧心。我想我是一个十足的宿命论者。无论发生什么，你都要勇敢面对。最重要的是，面对的时候别忘了要勇敢，要倾尽全力。

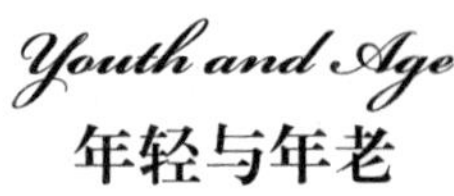

年轻与年老

◎ Robert Louis Stevenson

As we grow old, a sort of equable jog-trot of feeling is substituted for the violent ups and downs of passion and disgust; the same influence that restrains our hopes, quiets our **apprehensions**[①]; if the pleasures are less intense, the troubles are milder and more tolerable; and in a word, this period for which we are asked to hoard up everything as for a time of famine, is, in its own right, the richest, easiest, and happiest of life. Nay, by managing its own work and following its own happy inspiration, youth is doing the best it can to endow the leisure of age. A full, busy youth is your only prelude to a self-contained and independent age; and the muff inevitably develops into the bore. There are not many Doctor Johnsons, to set forth upon their first romantic voyage at sixty-four. If we wish to scale Mont Blanc or go down in a diving dress or up in a balloon, we must be about it while we are still young. It will not do to delay until we are clogged with prudence and limping with **rheumatism**[②] and people begin to ask us: "What does Gravity out of bed?" Youth is the time to go flashing from one end of the world to the other both in mind and body; to try the manners of different nations; to hear the chimes at midnight; to see sunrise in town and country; to be converted at a revival; to circumnavigate the metaphysics, write halting verses, run a mile to see a fire, and wait all day long in the theatre to applaud HERNANI.

---

① apprehension [ˌæpri'henʃən] n. 恐惧，忧虑，担心，挂念

② rheumatism ['ruːmətizəm] n. 风湿病

美丽语录

Go for the happy endings, because life doesn't have any sequels.

为了一个美丽的结果而努力吧，因为人生没有续集。

当我们慢慢变老时，一种平淡而缓慢的感觉代替了强烈的爱憎沉浮。同样，这种感觉让我们克制自己的希望，消除心中的忧虑。如果快乐不再那么热烈，那么烦恼就能变得微不足道，更容易忍受。总而言之，在这段时间里，我们必须备好一切，以备不时之需。这段时间是整个生命中最丰富多彩、最轻松、最幸福的。不但如此，通过管理自己的行为，随着快乐的灵感律动，年轻人尽力让自己的时代变得闲适安逸。充实忙碌的年轻时代是独立自主的老年生活的唯一前奏。而那些年轻时碌碌无为的人，他们的晚年注定是沉闷无聊的。世上的约翰逊博士并不多——在 64 岁那年才开启人生中的首次浪漫之旅。如果我们想要丈量勃朗峰，或者穿上潜水衣潜水，或者坐着热气球飞上高空，我们必须趁年轻时去做，不要拖到自己变得小心谨慎、腿脚不便时才去。那时，人们就会问我们："为何如此不安分？"年轻时代就是周游世界的时代，不论是精神游历还是身体力行；去体验不同国家的不同风情；去聆听午夜的钟声；去欣赏城市和乡间的日出；去为了重生而虔诚悔过；去博览玄学，写一些差强人意的诗句，跑一英里的路看篝火，等上一整天只是为了给《艾那尼》喝彩。

镌刻成长的印记

Life is tough, whether we want it to be or not. What we need to do is pray for roots that reach deep into the Eternal, so when the rains fall and the winds blow, we won't be swept asunder.

不管我们愿不愿意，生活总是艰难的。我们需要做的是祈祷深植我们的信念之根，这样，当面对风吹雨打时，我们就不会被伤害。

We're Just Beginning
从零开始

◎ Charles F. Kattering

"We are reading the first verse of the first chapter of a book whose pages are infinite..."

I do not know who wrote these words, but I have always liked them as a reminder that the future can be anything we want to make it. We can take the mysterious, hazy future and carve out of it anything that we can imagine, just as a **sculptor**① carves a statue from a shapeless stone.

We are all in the position of the farmer. If we plant a good seed, we reap a good harvest. If our seed is poor and full of weeds, we reap a useless crop. If we plant nothing at all, we harvest nothing at all.

I want the future to be better than the past. I don't want it **contaminated**② by the mistakes and errors with which history is filled. We should all be concerned about the future because that is where we will spend the remainder of our lives.

The past is gone and static. Nothing we can do will change it. The future is before us and dynamic. Everything we do will affect it. Each day brings with it new frontiers, in our homes and in our businesses, if we will only recognize them. We are just at the beginning of the progress in every field of human endeavor.

---

① sculptor ['skʌlptə] n. 雕刻家

② contaminated [kən'tæimineitid] adj. 弄脏的；受污染的；受毒害的

美丽语录

I am not afraid of tomorrow, for I have seen yesterday and love today.

我不害怕明天，因为我经历过昨天，又热爱今天。

“我们正在读一本书的第一章第一行，而这本书有无数页……”

我不知道这句话是谁写的，可我很喜欢。它提醒着我们，未来是由自己创造的，一切皆有可能。我们可以把神秘的、不可知的未来塑造成我们想象中的任何一种样子，就像雕塑家把一尊未成形的石头刻成雕像。

我们就像是农夫。如果我们播下良种，必将获得丰收。然而，如果播下劣种，或田间杂草丛生，我们收获的就是无用的庄稼。没有耕耘就不会有收获。

我希望未来比过去更加美好。我希望未来不再重蹈历史的错误与过失。我们应该专注于未来，因为我们的余生都将在未来中度过。

往昔已逝，静如止水，我们无力改变它。未来就在眼前，生机勃勃，我们所做的一切都会影响它。如果我们意识到这些，无论工作还是家庭，我们都能开拓一片新天地。在人类致力开拓的每一个领域里，我们正好站在进步的起跑点上。

What I Have Lived for

我为什么而活

◎ Bertrand Russell

Three passions, simple but overwhelmingly strong, have governed my life: the longing for love, the search for knowledge, and **unbearable**① pity for the suffering of mankind. These passions, like great winds, have blown me hither and thither, in a wayward course, over a deep ocean of anguish, reaching to the very verge of despair.

I have sought love, first, because it brings ecstasy—ecstasy so great that I would often have sacrificed all the rest of life for a few hours of this joy. I have sought it, next, because it relieves loneliness—that terrible loneliness in which one shivering consciousness looks over the rim of the world into the cold unfathomable lifeless abyss. I have sought it, finally, because in the union of love I have seen, in a mystic **miniature**②, the prefiguring vision of the heaven that saints and poets have imagined. This is what I sought, and though it might seem too good for human life, this is what—at last—I have found.

With equal passion I have sought knowledge. I have wished to understand

① unbearable ['n'bɛərəbl] adj. 不能忍受的；令人不能容忍的

② miniature ['miniətʃə] n. 缩样；小型物；小画像

美丽语录

Nobody can go back and start a new beginning, but anyone can start now and make a new ending.

没有人可以回到过去重新开始，但谁都可以从现在开始，书写一个全然不同的结局。

对爱情的渴望，对知识的探寻，对人类苦难无法遏制的同情，是支配我一生的单纯而强烈的三种情感。这些情感就像阵阵狂风，吹拂着四处飘零的我，有时甚至拂过痛苦的海洋，直抵绝望的边缘。

我渴望爱情，有三个原因。首先，爱情给我带来狂喜。这种狂喜是那样有力，我不惜抛弃余下的光阴，只为享受几个小时的爱给我带来的喜悦。其次，我一直在寻找它，因为爱情让我不再孤独。那个经历过可怕孤独的人，他总能穿过世界的边缘，看到冰冷的、无趣的、深不见底的深渊。最后，在我见过的爱的结合中，圣人和诗人所幻想的便是神秘的天堂缩影，这也正是我所追求的。虽然对一般人的生活而言，它有点太美好了，但这就是爱情最终帮我找到的东西。

我带着同样的情感探寻知识。我渴望读懂人类的心。我渴望知道为什么星星会发光。而且我还渴望了解毕达哥拉斯的力量。目前，我掌握的不多，就只有一些。

the hearts of men. I have wished to know why the stars shine. And I have tried to apprehend the Pythagorean power by which number holds sway above the flux. A little of this, but not much, have achieved.

Love and knowledge, so far as they were possible, led upward toward the heavens. But always pity brought me back to earth. Echoes of cries of pain **reverberate**[①] in my heart. Children in famine, victims tortured by oppressors, helpless old people a hated burden to their sons, and the whole world of loneliness, poverty, and pain make a mockery of what human life should be. I long to alleviate the evil, but I can't, and I too suffer.

This has been my life. I have found it worth living, and would gladly live it again if the chance were offered me.

① reverberate [ri'və:bəreit] v.（使）回响；（使）反射；（使）弹回

爱和知识尽可能地把我带上天堂，可我对人类的怜悯又将我拉回现实世界。痛苦的哭喊声时刻回荡在我的心间。饥荒中的孩童，受统治者压迫的受害者，被儿女视为负担的无助老人，还有全球普遍存在的孤单、贫困和痛苦，这一切的存在都是对人类理想生活的嘲讽。我希望自己有力量减轻这些痛苦，可我无能为力，因为我也是受害者之一。

也许这就是我的生活吧！我觉得活着是有意义的。如果再给我一次机会，我会欣然接受这个来之不易的重生的机会。

Kobe Bryant' Growing Road
科比·布莱恩特的成长之路

◎ Jr. Wall

Kobe Bryant first started turning heads on the basketball court when he was in middle school. His talents dominated the game so much that high schools from all over the Philadelphia area watched him grow up. The almost six-foot tall seventh grader definitely had the make-up and genes for the game, as his dad was former NBA forward, Joe Bryant. Kobe developed his basketball skills under the watchful eye of his father, helping his mission to become a professional basketball player. He worked daily on his game, watching video, playing in the playgrounds and listening to his father. When he entered high school at Lower Marion in Philadelphia, Kobe was a highly touted **recruit**[①]. He proved that he had the skills and work ethic to be a star at the next level and the scouts noticed this. Kobe didn't let anybody down either, as he played on the varsity basketball team his freshman year. He wouldn't immediately be a superstar, though. Rather it was the countless hours of early morning workouts by himself in the gymnasium that escalated Kobe's talents.

Kobe became a better player every year he played at Lower Marion and

① recruit [ri'kru:t] v. 征募（新兵）；吸收（新成员）；雇用

美丽语录

I can accept failure but I can't accept not trying.

我可以接受失败，但绝对不能接受自己都未曾奋斗过。

科比・布莱恩特上中学的时候才真正在篮球场上崭露头角。他有着惊人的篮球天赋，所以费城所有高中都在关注他的成长。这个七年级时就长到近6英尺的小学生，毫无疑问就是为篮球而生的，就像他的爸爸乔伊・布莱恩特——曾经在NBA征战数年的前锋一样。科比在父亲的关注下训练篮球技巧，并在父亲的帮助下完成了自己的使命——成为一个职业篮球运动员。他每天都在为比赛做准备：看录像、到球场上练球、聆听父亲的教诲。当他进入费城的一所高中——劳尔梅里恩时，他就成了最受瞩目的新生。他证明了自己拥有成为下一颗新星的实力和职业道德，并且球探也发现了这一点。科比高中一年级时就加入了学校代表队，虽然他无法一夜之间成为一个超级巨星，但他不会让任何人失望。每天清晨，健身房里那无数个小时的体能测验，让他能够更好地施展自己的才华。

科比在劳尔梅里恩打球的那几年，他就是一个出色的球员，并且很快

soon enough, he had developed into one of the **premier**[1] talents at the high school level. He sold out the games everywhere he played during his junior and senior years and he didn't disappoint anyone. He once packed the school gym so much that it caused a traffic jam on the main highway just outside the school.

He went on to finish his high school career as the all-time leading point scorer in Pennsylvania history with a total of 2,883 points. Kobe's highly decorated high school career made him the 13th overall choice by the Charlotte Hornets in the 1996NBA draft.

① premier ['premjə] adj. 第一的，首要的

成为高中时代最具才华的球员之一。大学三年级和四年级时，凡是他参加的球赛，场场爆满。当然，他也没有让任何人失望。有一次，学校体育馆内挤满了来看他比赛的人，因此造成了学校外主要高速公路的交通堵塞。

高中毕业时，他以惊人的 2883 分创造了宾州高校的得分纪录。科比充满荣誉的高中时代让他成为了第 13 位被夏洛特黄蜂队挑中的球员，直接从高中进入了 1996 年 NBA 选秀。

The Road Not Taken
未选择的路

◎ Robert Frost

Two roads diverged in a yellow wood,
And sorry I could not travel both
And be one traveler, long I stood
And looked down one as far as I could
To where it bent in the undergrowth;

Then took the other, as just as fair,
And having perhaps the better claim,
Because it was grassy and wanted wear;
Though as for that the passing there
Had worn them really about the same,

And both that morning equally lay
In leaves no step had trodden black.
Oh, I kept the first for another day!
Yet knowing how way leads on to way,

美丽语录

I don't regret the things I've done, I regret the things I didn't do when I had the chance.

我不为做过的事而懊悔。我只是遗憾，有些事，有机会却没有去做。

黄色的树林里分出两条路
可惜我无法同时走过
独自旅行，我久久伫立于路口
我向着一条路极目望去
直到它消失在丛林深处

可我选择了另外一条路
它荒草丛生，寂静悠远
显得更美丽诱人
虽然这两条路上
都很少留下旅人的足迹

那天清晨，落叶飘满地
但两条路上都未见脚印
噢！另一条路，改日再见
我深知道路绵延无尽头

I doubted if I should ever come back.

I shall be telling this with a sigh
Somewhere ages and ages hence:
Two roads diverged in a wood, and I—
I took the one less traveled by,
And that has made all the difference.

恐怕我难以重返

我想我会在多年以后
一边叹息，一边回忆
树林里分出两条路——
我选了人迹罕至的那条
从此有了不同的人生

Flying Youth
转眼青春的散场

◎ Doris

"Youth" seems to be fading away in my life, only leaving me some unforgettable and cherished memories. Something that we used to think would last forever in our lives, had actually vanished in a second before we realized it. Those who we used to deeply love or miss, have now become the most acquainted strangers. Our once pure and beautiful dream, is gradually fading away with time passing by... This is youth, which is indeed an endless cycle from familiarity to strangeness, and from strangeness to familiarity, until the curtain of our youth is closing off little by little, along with our childish fantasies.

Human is such a strange animal that when we mostly did not cherish something until we lost it. We have gained a lot of things, but also lost a lot. What we want is merely getting the peace of mind. We care for children because they are the most pure-minded and kind-hearted among human beings. We are fond of staying with the old, because we can sense their inner peace from their serene faces. Maybe for them, the essence of life is to live it in the most comfortable way they deem. We may also love cats because their relaxation renders us a substantive sense of life.

美丽语录

Life isn't always beautiful, but the struggles make you stronger, the changes make you wiser.

生活不一定是一直美好的，但是那些挣扎可以让你变得更坚强，那些改变可以让你变得更有智慧。

"青春"这个字眼仿佛在我的生命中消失了，只留下一些难忘的美好回忆。我们总以为青春是生命中永远不会消失的东西，可它总是在我们意识到之前便转瞬即逝了。那些我们曾经深爱过或思念过的人，已经变成了最熟悉的陌生人。我们曾经拥有的纯洁而美好的梦，随着时间的推移，也慢慢地消失了……这就是青春，一个从熟悉到陌生，又从陌生到熟悉的无限循环，直到你的青春伴随着孩童的幻想一点一点消失。

人类是种很奇怪的动物，我们总是在失去之后才懂得珍惜。我们获得了许多，也失去了许多。我们渴望的仅仅是心灵的平静。我们喜爱孩子，因为他们是最纯真、最善良的人。我们享受和老人共度的时光，因为他们安祥的脸庞让你感觉到他们内心的平静。也许对他们来说，生活的本质就是用最舒心的方式热爱生活。也许我们也会喜欢猫，因为它们悠闲自在，有一份真实感。

生命里有太多容易消失和破碎的东西。因此，我们要逐渐学会淡然地面对一切。也许，我们时常更愿意相信自己，而非相信或依靠别人，因为

There are many things in our lives that are easily gone or broken. Therefore, we will gradually learn to become **apathetic**[①] and indifferent towards everything. Maybe oftentimes, we are inclined to believe in ourselves rather than trust and rely on others, because in our lives, nothing will stay with us eternally and all will be gone one day eventually. Sometimes it is not the world that abandons us, but we who abandon the world. It can be evidenced by the fact that we have learnt to deny something habitually and therefore lost a lot of things. More often than not, we would believe that it is life that hurts us rather than believe that it is our personality flaw that hurts ourselves.

We are in **strenuous**[②] effort in changing our fate, bringing more happiness to people around us, realizing our dreams and reaching the love we are anticipating. However, we soon realize it is by no means easy to achieve any of them. It is a lifelong commitment and many things would alter with time and no one can guarantee eternity. Hence, silence becomes the best solution to all difficulties and hardships. Since we cannot make a for-sure promise, why do we still bother to boast too much about it? We still need to get down to our business with our own effort.

The flying youth has deposited too many things in our heart. Life should be treated with special care like an egg in your hands. We should treasure every moment of sincerity and gratefulness because the best things will be gone very easily. Try to forgive every lie simply because everyone has ever lied sometime. If you do not want to have tearing eyes, then just try to smile and hold a positive attitude towards your life every day!

---

① apathetic [ˌæpə'θetik] adj. 冷淡的；无动于衷的

② strenuous ['strenjuəs] adj. 费劲的；奋发的；强烈的；紧张的

在我们的生命中，没有什么会永远追随我们，最终，一切都将离我们而去。有时，不是世界抛弃了我们，而是我们抛弃了世界。我们学会了习惯性地说不，从而与许多东西擦肩而过。很多时候，我们宁愿相信是生活伤害了我们，也不愿相信是我们的个性缺失伤害了自己。

我们千方百计地想要改变命运，想要给周遭的人带来更多的快乐，想要实现我们的梦想，想要拥有一份期盼已久的感情。然而我们很快就意识到，实现以上任何一点都不是件简单的事。这是一件需要努力一辈子的事情，因为很多东西会随着时间而改变，没有人能够保证永恒。所以，有的时候，沉默便是战胜困难艰辛的最好方式。既然我们承诺不了，又何必多说呢？实现一切靠的还是自己的努力。

飞逝的青春留给我们太多的东西。生活就像是捧在手心里的鸡蛋，需要特别的照料。我们要珍惜每一份真诚和感动，因为最好的东西总是很容易流逝。试着原谅每一个谎言吧！因为每个人都曾在某时说过谎。如果你不忍心看到一双噙满泪水的双眼，那就微笑吧！抱着一种乐观向上的态度对待生命中的每一天！

The Boy Under the Tree

树下的男孩

◎ David Coleman & Kevin Randall

In the summer recess between freshman and **sophomore**① years in college, I was invited to be an instructor at a high school leadership camp hosted by a college in Michigan. I was already highly involved in most campus activities, and I jumped at the opportunity.

About an hour into the first day of camp, amid the frenzy of icebreakers and forced interactions, I first noticed the boy under the tree. He was small and skinny, and his obvious discomfort and shyness made him appear frail and fragile. Only fifty feet away, two hundred eager campers were bumping bodies, playing, joking and meeting each other, but the boy under the tree seemed to want to be anywhere other than where he was. The desperate loneliness he radiated almost stopped me from approaching him, but I remembered the instructions from the senior staff to stay alert for campers who might feel left out.

As I walked toward him, I said, "I, my name is Kevin, and I'm one of the counselors. It's nice to meet you. How are you?" In a shaky, sheepish voice he reluctantly answered, "Okay, I guess." I calmly asked him if he wanted to join the activities and meet some new people. He quietly replied, "No, this is not really my thing."

---

① sophomore ['sɔfəmɔː] n.（大学，高中的）二年级学生

美丽语录

You make millions of decisions that mean nothing and then one day your order takes out and it changes your life.

你每天都在做很多看起来毫无意义的决定，但某天你的某个决定就能改变你的一生。

在大一生活结束的那个暑假，我受邀到密歇根州一所大学主办的高中领导才能夏令营担任辅导员一职。我参加过许多大学举办的活动，于是便欣然接受了这次邀请。

夏令营的第一天，我花了一个小时来缓和气氛，强迫大家进行互动。那时我第一次注意到那个树下的男孩。他又小又瘦，明显的不安和羞怯让他看起来更加弱不经风。离他只有 50 英尺远的地方，两百个狂热的露营爱好者正在蹦蹦跳跳地闹着说着，互相结识。可那个树下的男孩看样子只要不待在这里，去哪儿都可以。他表现出令人绝望的孤寂，仿佛要拒我于之千里之外。这时，我想起那些资深辅导员给我的提醒——给那些可能感到被忽略的队员一些特殊关注。

我朝他走去，说道："你好，我叫凯文，我是夏令营的辅导员。很高兴见到你。你好吗？"他用颤抖羞怯的声音不情愿地回答道，"还好吧。"我冷静地问他是否愿意参加一些活动，结交一些新朋友。他静静地答道："不，

I could sense that he was in a new world, that this whole experience was foreign to him. But I somehow knew it wouldn't be right to push him, either. He didn't need a pep talk; he needed a friend. After several silent moments, my first interaction with the boy under the tree was over.

At lunch the next day, I found myself leading camp songs at the top of my lungs for two hundred of my new friends. The campers eagerly participated. My gaze wandered over the mass of noise and movement and was caught by the image of the boy from under the tree, sitting alone, staring out the window. I nearly forgot the words to the song I was supposed to be leading. At my first opportunity, I tried again, with the same questions as before, "How are you doing? Are you okay?" To which he again replied, "Yeah, I'm all right. I just don't really get into this stuff." As I left the cafeteria, I realized this was going to take more time and effort than I had thought—if it was even possible to get through to him at all.

That evening at our nightly staff meeting, I made my concerns about him known. I explained to my fellow staff members my impression of him and asked them to pay special attention and spend time with him when they could.

The days I spend at camp each year fly by faster than any others I have known. Thus, before I knew it, mid-week had dissolved into the final night of camp, and I was **chaperoning**[①] the "last dance". The students were doing all they could to savor every last moment with their new "best friends"—friends they would probably never see again.

As I watched the campers share their parting moments, I suddenly saw what would be one of the most vivid memories of my life. The boy from under the

① chaperon ['ʃæpərəun] v. 陪伴；护送

这真的不是我想做的事情。”

我能感觉到，他处在一个崭新的世界里，这里的一切对他来说都是陌生的。可是，我有时觉得强迫他也不是什么好办法。他需要的不是鼓励的话语，而是一位朋友。一段沉默过后，我和树下男孩的第一次互动也宣告结束了。

第二天午餐的时候，我为两百位新朋友高声唱起了夏令营之歌。队员们兴高采烈地跟着我一起唱。我的目光穿过嘈杂流动的人群，停在了那个单独坐在树下凝望着窗外的男孩身上。我差点忘了正在领唱的歌词。我又抓住机会试着再一次接近他，我像上一次那样问道：“你感觉怎么样？你还好吗？”他还是那样回答我：“是的，我还好。我只是不太想做这些事情。”从餐厅走出来的时候，我明白了，要想打开他的心扉，需要的时间和精力比我之前预计的还要多。

那天晚上，在全体工作人员例行会议上，我说出了对他的忧虑。我向我的同事说明了我对他的印象，并且请他们多留意他，多抽点时间陪他。

每一年我在夏令营的日子，比我所知道的其他任何时候都要过得快。于是不知不觉，周三成为了此次夏令营的最后一夜，我陪伴着他们跳最后一支舞。学生们和新交的“挚友”——或许今后再也无法相见的朋友——尽情享受这最后时刻。

正当我看着队员们共享临别时刻时，我突然看见了生命中最动人的一

tree, who had stared blankly out the kitchen window, was now a shirtless dancing wonder. He owned the dance floor as he and two girls proceeded to cut a rug. I watched as he shared meaningful, intimate time with people at whom he couldn't even look just days earlier. I couldn't believe it was the same person.

In October of my sophomore year, a late-night phone call pulled me away from my chemistry book. A soft-spoken, unfamiliar voice asked politely, "Is Kevin there?"

"You're talking to him, who's this?"

"This is Tom Johnson's mom. Do you remember Tommy from leadership camp?"

The boy under the tree. How could I not remember?

"Yes, I do." I said. "He's a very nice young man. How is he?"

An abnormally long pause followed, then Mrs. Johnson said, "My Tommy was walking home from school this week when he was hit by a car and killed." Shocked, I offered my **condolences**①.

"I just wanted to call you," she said, "because Tommy mentioned you so many times. I wanted you to know that he went back to school this fall with confidence. He made new friends. His grades went up. And he even went out on a few dates. I just wanted to thank you for making a difference for Tom. The last few months were the best few months of his life."

In that instant, I realized how easy it is to give a bit of yourself every day. You may never know how much each gesture may mean to someone else. I tell this story as often as I can, and when I do, I urge others to look out for their own "boy under the tree".

---

① condolence [kən'dəuləns] n. 吊辞；慰问

幕：那个曾经茫然凝望着厨窗外的树下男孩，此时早已脱去外上衣，正在热情地舞蹈着。当他和两个女孩一起热舞时，他吸引了全场的目光。我看着他与人分享着意义深长又亲密无间的时光。可就在几天前，他甚至都不愿意看这些人一眼，我简直不敢相信这是同一个人。

大二那年 10 月的一个深夜，我放下手中的化学书，接了一个电话。听筒里传来一个陌生、温柔、彬彬有礼的声音："您是凯文吗？"

"我是。请问哪位？"

"我是汤姆·约翰逊的妈妈。您还记得参加过领导才能夏令营的汤米吗？"

那个树下男孩，我怎么会不记得呢?

"当然，"我说，"他是个非常不错的年轻人。他还好吗？"

很长的停顿后，约翰逊夫人接着说："这周我的汤米在回家的路上被车撞了，就那样走了。"我震惊极了，并请她节哀。

"我只是想打个电话给你，"她说，"因为汤米曾多次向我提起你。我想让你知道，这个秋天，他信心满满地回到学校，结交了新朋友，学习成绩也提高了，甚至还和女孩子约会了几次。我想谢谢你，是你改变了汤姆。这最后几个月是他生命里最灿烂的时光。"

刹那间，我明白了：每天奉献一点点是件很容易的事，可你也许永远不会知道，每一个善意的小举动会给别人带来多大的影响。我无数次说起这个故事，我这么做就是为了让更多的人留意他们自己的那个"树下男孩"。

Growing in the Middle Ground
在探索中成长

◎ Anne Phipps

I believe that my beliefs are changing. Nothing is positive. Perhaps I am in a stage of metamorphosis which will one day have me emerging complete, sure of everything. Perhaps I shall spend my life searching.

Until this winter, I believed in **outward**[1] things, in beauty as I found it in nature and art. Beauty passed, swift and sure, from the outside to the inside, bringing intense emotion. I felt a formless faith when I rode through summer woods, when I heard the counterpoint of breaking waves, when I held a flower in my hand. There was the same inspiration from art—here and there, in flashes—in seeing for the first time the delicacy of a white jade vase, or the rich beauty of a rug, in hearing a passage of music played almost perfectly, in watching Markova dance Giselle, most of all in reading. Other people's consciousness, their sensitivity to emotion, color, sound, their feeling for form, instructed me. The necessity for beauty I found to be the highest good, the human soul's greatest gift. It was not, I felt, all.

This winter I came to college. The questions put to me changed. Lists of

① outward ['autwəd] adj. 外表的，表面的；外界的

美丽语录

Life is not always what we want it to be. We fight. We cry. And sometimes, we give up. But in our hearts, we know it's still love.

生活有时不尽如人意。我们挣扎、哭泣，有时甚至放弃。但内心始终要充满爱。

我坚信自己的信仰一直在改变。凡事无绝对。或许，我还在发育阶段，总有一天我会发育完全，从而坚信一切。或许，我将要用一生的时间去探寻。

这个冬季以前，我信仰外界的事物，相信从大自然和艺术中发现的美。可美总是转瞬即逝，留下的只是无尽感伤。当我骑马穿过夏日的丛林，当我侧耳倾听浪花翻滚的声音，当我手持一朵鲜花时，我就能感觉到一种无形的信念。艺术也能带来同样的灵感，它无所不在，稍纵即逝——就像我第一次看见一个精美的白玉花瓶或一块华丽的地毯，听到一段演奏得近乎完美的音乐，看到马尔科娃在《吉赛尔》中的优美舞姿，我都能感觉到这种灵感。然而，这种灵感绝大部分源自阅读。他人的思想，他们对于情感、颜色、声音的敏感，以及对形式的感知，都能给我以启迪。我发现，对美的需求是人类最崇高的举动，是人类灵魂最伟大的天赋。可我觉得，它并非一切。

今年冬天，我上大学了。我所面临的问题也改变了。很多事实和那些

facts and "who dragged whom how many times around the walls of what?" lost importance. Instead I was asked eternal questions: What is Beauty? What is Truth? What is God? I talked about faith with other students. I read St. Augustine and Tolstoy. I wondered if I hadn't been **worshiping**① around the edges. Nature and art were the edges, an inner faith was the center. I discovered, really discovered, that I had a soul. Just sitting in the sun one day, I realized the shattering meaning of St. Augustine's statement that the sun and the moon, all the wonders of nature, are not God's "first works", but second to the spiritual works.

I had, up till then, perceived spiritual beauty, only through the outward; it had come into me. Now, I am **groping**② towards an inner spiritual consciousness that will be able to go out from me. I am lost in the middle ground; I am learning.

① worship ['wə:ʃip] v. 信仰，崇敬
② grope [grəup] v. 探索，探求

“多少次谁拉着谁围绕着哪面墙徘徊？”早已不再重要。相反，一些永恒的问题开始困扰着我：什么是美？什么是真理？什么是上帝？我曾和其他学生讨论过信仰的问题。我读过圣·奥古斯丁与托尔斯泰的著作。我想知道，自己是否一直徘徊在信仰的边缘。自然和艺术都是边缘，内心的信仰才是核心。我发现了，真的发现了，自己拥有一个灵魂。有一天，当我坐在阳光下时，我终于明白了圣·奥古斯丁说过的那句话：太阳和月亮，所有自然界的奇迹，都不是上帝的“初作”，而是精神上的二次创造。

直到那一刻，我才能看透外界事物，欣赏到精神上的美。那种美已然住进我心里。现在，我正在通往内心精神世界的道路上摸索前行着。我迷失在探索之中。我正在学习。

Brush Past the Death

与死神擦肩而过

◎ Steve Jobs

When I was 17, I read a quote that went something like: "If you live each day as if it was your last, someday you'll most certainly be right." It made an impression on me, and since then, for the past 33 years, I have looked in the mirror every morning and asked myself: "If today were the last day of my life, would I want to do what I am about to do today?" And whenever the answer has been "No" for too many days in a row, I know I need to change something.

Remembering that I'll be dead soon is the most important tool I've ever encountered to help me make the big choices in life. Because almost everything—all external expectations, all pride, all fear of embarrassment or failure—these things just fall away in the face of death, leaving only what is truly important. Remembering that you are going to die is the best way I know to avoid the trap of thinking you have something to lose. You are already naked. There is no reason not to follow your heart.

About a year ago, I was **diagnosed**① with cancer. I had a scan at 7:30 in the morning, and it clearly showed a tumor on my pancreas. I didn't even know what a pancreas was. The doctors told me this was almost certainly a type of

---

① diagnose ['daiəgnəuz] v. 诊断

美丽语录

Never underestimate your power to change yourself.

永远不要低估你改变自我的能力！

我 17 岁的时候，读过一句格言，好像是这样说的："如果你把每一天都当作最后一天去生活的话，总有一天，你会觉得自己这么做是正确的。"这句话给我留下了深刻印象。从那以后，在过去的 33 年中，每天清晨我都会对着镜子问自己："如果今天是我生命中的最后一天，那我还会去做原先计划好的那些事情吗？"可连续多日我得到的答案都是"不会"。于是，我明白我该做些改变了。

时刻提醒自己我即将死去，是帮我做出人生许多重大抉择的重要工具。因为几乎所有的一切——一切外来的期望、一切骄傲、一切关乎面子和失败的恐惧——在死亡面前，这些东西都将消失殆尽，留下的只是真正重要的东西。时刻提醒自己我即将死去，是不让自己陷入患得患失的最好办法。因为此时的你已然一无所有了，就没有理由不顺从你的心。

大约在一年前，我被诊断出患有癌症。我在早上 7 点半做了扫描，扫描结果清楚地显示我的胰腺上长了一个肿瘤。当时，我甚至都不知道胰腺是什么东西。医生很肯定地告诉我，我得的是一种基本上无法治愈的癌症。

cancer that is incurable, and that I should expect to live no longer than three to six months. My doctor advised me to go home and get my affairs in order, which is doctor's code for preparing yourself to die. It means to try to tell your kids everything you thought you'd have the next 10 years to tell them in just a few months. It means to make sure everything is buttoned up so that it will be as easy as possible for your family. It means to say your goodbyes.

I lived with that diagnosis all day. Later that evening I had a biopsy, where they stuck an endoscope down my throat, through my stomach and into my intestines, put a needle into my pancreas and got a few cells from the tumor. I was sedated, but my wife, who was there, told me that when they viewed the cells under a microscope the doctors started crying because it turned out to be a very rare form of pancreatic cancer that is curable with surgery. I had the surgery and I'm fine now.

This was the closest I've been to facing death, and I hope it's the closest I get for a few more decades. Having lived through it, I can now say this to you with a bit more certainty than when death was a useful but purely intellectual concept:

No one wants to die. Even people who want to go to heaven don't want to die to get there. And yet death is the destination we all share. No one has ever escaped it. And that is as it should be, because Death is very likely the single best invention of Life. It is Life's change agent. It clears out the old to make way for the new. Right now the new is you, but someday not too long from now, you will gradually become the old and be cleared away. Sorry to be so dramatic, but it is quite true.

Your time is limited, so don't waste it living someone else's life. Don't be

我活在世上的日子可能不会超过 3 到 6 个月。我的医生建议我回家，安排好后事，这是医生们专门对等死的病人说的话。这也就是意味着，你要把本来打算在未来 10 年内对孩子们说的话，在这几个月里说完；意味着你要把一切安排妥当，让你的家人尽可能地轻松些；意味着你就要说“再见”了。

那一整天我都在想着我的诊断结果。那天夜里晚些时候，我做了活组织切片检查。医生把一个内窥镜从我的喉咙伸进去，通过我的胃，进入我的肠子，然后用一根针刺进我的胰腺，在肿瘤上取出一些细胞。我被注射了镇定剂。可当时也在场的妻子后来告诉我，当医生用显微镜观察这些细胞时，突然大叫了起来。原来我患的是一种罕见的、可以用手术治愈的胰腺癌。于是，我做了手术，现在痊愈了。

那就是我和死神擦肩而过的一次，我希望这也是接下来几十年最接近死神的一次。以前死亡对我来说只是一个有用却纯粹是理论上的概念，可有了这次经历之后，我可以更加确信地对你们说：

没有人会想死，即使人们想上天堂，也不会为了去那儿而去死。然而，死亡是我们的最终归宿，没有人能够逃脱。也许就该如此，因为死亡是生命唯一的最好发明。它是生命不断变化的源动力。它除旧呈新。如今，你们是新人，然后不久之后，你们也会慢慢变老，接着被淘汰。我很抱歉如此戏剧性，但事实就是如此。

trapped by dogma—which is living with the results of other people's thinking. Don't let the noise of others' opinions drown out[1] your own inner voice. And most important, have the courage to follow your heart and intuition. They somehow already know what you truly want to become. Everything else is secondary.

① drown out 压过，盖过

你的时间有限，所以不要把时间浪费在重复别人的生活上。不要受教条的束缚，不然你就只能按照别人的思想生活。不要让别人纷乱的意见淹没你内心的呼声。最重要的是，要勇于听从你内心的直觉。因为内心的直觉已然知道你想要成为什么样的人。其他的一切都是次要的。

The Fork in the Road

面对人生的十字路口

◎ Florence Scovel Shinn

Every day there is a necessity of choice (a fork in the road). "Shall I do this, or shall I do that? Shall I go, or shall I stay?" Many people do not know what to do. They rush about letting other people make decisions for them, then regret having taken their advice.

There are others who carefully reason things out. They weigh and measure the situation like dealing in **groceries**①, and are surprised when they fail to obtain their goal.

There are still other people who follow the magic path of intuition and find themselves in their Promised Land in the twinkling of an eye.

Intuition is a spiritual faculty high above the reasoning mind, but on the path is all that you desire or require. So choose ye this day to follow the magic path of intuition.

In most people it is a faculty which has remained dormant. So we say, "Awake though that sleeps. Wake up to your leads and **hunches**②!"

---

① grocery ['grəusəri] n. 杂货店

② hunch [hʌntʃ] n. 直觉，预感

美丽语录

Make up your mind to act decidedly and take the consequences. No good is ever done in this world by hesitation.

下定决心，果断行动，并承担后果。在这世界上犹豫不决成就不了任何事。

我们每天都要面临不同的选择（面对人生的十字路口）。“是该这样，还是该那样？我是该走还是该留？”许多人都很茫然不知所措，所以他们急着让别人为自己拿主意，接着再为听了他人的意见而后悔。

一些人总是小心翼翼地为未来计划着。他们就像经营杂货店那样经营着自己的未来。可是，当他们无法达到自己的目标时，往往又会惊叹不已。

还有一些人会跟着直觉走，发现自己转眼之间就到了梦想中的天堂。

直觉，是一种高于理性思想的本能。然而，只有当你充满强烈欲望或迫切需求时，这种本能才会显现出来。所以，相信你的直觉，跟着感觉走吧！

但是，大多数人身上的这种本能都还未被唤醒。所以，我们要说：“唤醒沉睡的直觉吧，唤醒心中的巨人吧！”

现在，你必须作出选择，你面对着人生的十字路口。向你的直觉索要

Now it is necessary for you to make a decision, you face a fork in the road. Ask for a definite unmistakable lead, and you will receive it.

So we find we have success through being strong and very courageous in following spiritual law.

A well-known man, who has become a great power in the financial world, said to a friend, "I always follow intuition and I am luck incarnate."

Inspirations are the most important thing in life. People come to truth meetings for inspiration. I find the right word will start **divine**[①] activity operating in their affairs.

In every act prompted by fear lies the germ of its own defeat.

① divine [di'vain] adj. 天赐的；神圣的；非凡的，天才的

一个确定答案吧！然后，勇敢地接受它！

于是我们发现，成功路上有了直觉相伴，我们变得更加强大，更加勇敢了。

一位金融界的知名成功人士对他的朋友说：“我一直跟着感觉走，我是一个幸运儿。”

灵感是人的一生中最重要的东西。人们往往会产生灵感。有了灵感，人们在工作时就能如鱼得水，得心应手了。

无论何时，都不要惧怕，因为它会在你心底生根发芽。

Growing Roots
成长的树根

© Philip Gulley

When I was growing up, I had an old neighbor named Dr. Gibbs. He didn't look like any doctor I'd ever known. He never yelled at us for playing in his yard. I remember him as someone who was a lot nicer than circumstances warranted.

When Dr. Gibbs wasn't saving lives, he was planting trees. His house sat on ten acres, and his life's goal was to make it a forest.

The good doctor had some interesting theories concerning plant husbandry. He came from the "No pain, no gain" school of **horticulture**[①]. He never watered his new trees, which flew in the face of conventional wisdom. Once I asked why. He said that watering plants spoiled them, and that if you water them, each successive tree generation will grow weaker and weaker. So you have to make things rough for them and weed out the weenie trees early on.

He talked about how watering trees made for shallow roots, and how trees that weren't watered had to grow deep roots in search of moisture. I took him to mean that deep roots were to be treasured.

So he never watered his trees. He'd plant an oak and, instead of watering

① horticulture ['hɔːtikʌltʃə] n. 园艺；园艺术

美丽语录

Don't pray for easy lives. Pray to be stronger men.

不要祈祷生活的舒适，应该祈祷自己变得更加坚强。

在我还是孩子的时候，我有一个老邻居叫吉布斯医生。他不像我认识的任何一个医生。我们在他的院子里玩耍，他从来不骂我们。我记得他是一个非常和蔼的人。

吉布斯医生不去拯救生命的时候，就会去种植树木。他的住所占地 10 英亩，他的人生目标就是将它变成一片森林。

这个好心的医生对于植物畜牧业有一番有趣的理论。他来自一个“不劳无获”的园艺学校。他从不给他新种的树浇水，这显然有悖于常理。有一次我问为什么，他说浇水会宠坏了它们，如果浇水，每一棵成活的树的后代会变得越来越娇弱。所以，你必须让它们的生长环境变得艰苦些，尽早淘汰那些弱不禁风的树。

他还告诉我用水浇灌的树的根是如何浅，而那些没有浇水的树的根就必须深深扎进泥土深处搜寻水分。我将他的话理解为：深根是十分宝贵的。

所以他从不给他的树浇水。他种了一棵橡树，每天早上，非但不给它浇水，还用一张卷起的报纸抽打它。“啪！噼！砰！”我问他为什么这样

it every morning, he'd beat it with a rolled-up newspaper. Smack! Slap! Pow! I asked him why he did that, and he said it was to get the tree's attention.

Dr. Gibbs went to glory a couple of years after I left home. Every now and again, I walked by his house and looked at the trees that I'd watched him plant some twenty-five years ago. They're granite strong now. Big and robust. Those trees wake up in the morning and beat their chests and drink their coffee black.

I planted a couple of trees a few years back. Carried water to them for a solid summer. Sprayed them. Prayed over them. The whole nine yards. Two years of coddling has resulted in trees that expect to be waited on hand and foot. Whenever a cold wind blows in, they tremble and chatter their branches. Sissy trees.

Funny things about those trees of Dr. Gibbs'. Adversity and **deprivation**[①] seemed to benefit them in ways comfort and ease never could.

Every night before I go to bed, I check on my two sons. I stand over them and watch their little bodies, the rising and falling of life within. I often pray for them. Mostly I pray that their lives will be easy. But lately I've been thinking that it's time to change my prayer.

This change has to do with the inevitability of cold winds that hit us at the core. I know my children are going to encounter hardship, and I'm praying they won't be naive. There's always a cold wind blowing somewhere.

So I'm changing my prayer. Because life is tough, whether we want it to be or not. Too many times we pray for ease, but that's a prayer seldom met. What we need to do is pray for roots that reach deep into the Eternal, so when the rains fall and the winds blow, we won't be swept asunder.

---

① deprivation [ˌdepriˈveiʃən] n. 剥夺；免职；损失

做，他说这是为了引起树的注意。

在我离开家两年后，吉布斯医生就去世了。每一次，我走过他的房子时，就会看看那些 25 年前我曾看着他种下的那些树。如今它们已像岩石般硬朗了。枝繁叶茂，生气勃勃。这些树在早晨醒过来，拍打着胸脯，啜饮着苦难的汁水。

几年前，我也曾种下两三棵树。整整一个夏天我都坚持为它们浇水。给它们喷杀虫剂，为它们祈祷。整整九平方码大的地方。结果，两年的溺爱使这两棵树弱不禁风。每当寒风吹起，它们就颤抖起来，枝叶直打颤。娇里娇气的树。

吉布斯医生的树真是有趣。逆境和折磨带给它们的益处，似乎是舒适和安逸永远都无法给予的。

每天晚上睡觉前，我都要看看两个儿子。我俯视着他们那幼小的身体，生命就在其中起落沉浮。我经常为他们祈祷，祈祷他们的生活能一帆风顺。但近来，我想是时候该改变我的祈祷词了。

这种改变与寒风将不可避免地直击我们的要害。我知道我的孩子们会遇到困难，我祈祷他们不会幼稚而脆弱。某些地方总会有寒风吹过。

所以，我改变了我的祈祷词。因为无论我们愿不愿意，生活总是艰难的。我们已祈祷了太多的安逸，但却少有实现。我们所要做的是祈祷深植我们的信念之根，这样，当雨落风吹时，我们就不会被伤害。

踏上梦想的舞台

⊙ *There's never a perfect age to live your dreams. The perfect age is right now.*

⊙ *Make your goal known. Travel one step at a time.*

⊙ *Keep your dream alive. Long-term goals exist because they take a long time.*

⊙ 根本没有所谓的实现梦想的理想年龄。最佳时机就是立刻开始。

⊙ 明确你的目标，一步一个脚印。

⊙ 让你的梦想永远充满活力。长期的目标需要长时间的努力。

It's Never Too Late For Success

成功之路，永不言迟

◎ Charles D. Rice

You and your parents can stop worrying—Edison, Darwin and lots more were far from being geniuses in their teens.

History books seldom mention it, but the truth is that many of our greatest figures were practically "beatniks" when they were teenagers. They were given to daydreaming, indecision, **hebetudes**① (plain dullness), and they showed no promise of being a doctor, lawyer or teacher.

So, young men and women, if you suffer from the same symptoms, don't despair. The world was built by men and women whose parents worried that they would "never amount to a hill of beans". You don't hear too much about their early failures because parents prefer to cite more inspiring examples.

A MAN THEY DON'T TELL YOU ABOUT

If you take piano lessons and your attitude towards practicing is marked by laziness, your parents might justly complain and flaunt before you the famous picture of little Mozart in his ruffled night-shirt, playing the piano at midnight in

① hebetude ['hebitju:d] n. 迟钝；愚钝

美丽语录

You got a dream, you gotta protect it. People can't do something themselves, they wanna tell you that you can't do it. If you want something, go get it.

如果你有梦想，守护它。当人们做不到一些事情的时候，他们就会说你也同样不能。既然有了目标，你就要努力实现。

你和你的父母可以不必担忧了——爱迪生、达尔文还有许多其他人在他们年少时远非天才。

历史书上很少提到这些，但事实是：我们许多伟人在他们青少年时是“垮掉的一代”。他们也会做白日梦，也会优柔寡断，也会犯傻。而且，他们身上也没有显现出能够成为医生、律师或教师的潜质。

所以，年轻的男女们，如果你们遇到了同样的状况，不必绝望。这个世界就是由那些父母担心会一事无成的男男女女创造的。他们早年失败的事情，想必你很少听说，因为父母更喜欢引用更多鼓舞人心的例子。

他们不向你谈起的一个人

如果你正在学钢琴，可你并不勤于练习。这时，你的父母可能会一边指责你，一边在你面前对着一张著名的画尽情夸耀——穿着睡袍的小莫扎特大半夜还在阁楼上练钢琴。可关键是，你的父母不会给你看另外一副

the attic. But the point is, your parents would not show you a picture of a certain part who never showed a whit of interest in music during his formative years. In fact he never showed talent in any direction whatever. Finally put to studying law, he barely passed his final exams. It was not until he was 22 that he suddenly became fired with a great passion for music and his name was Peter Ilyich Tchaikovsky.

EDISON WAS "ADDLED"

In the sciences, there have been hundreds of geniuses who aimed straight at the goal from their earliest years, and hundreds who showed no aptitude at all. So it goes. You have the Wright Brothers, who were brilliant in engineering in their early teens, and you have Thomas Alva Edison, whose teacher tried to get him out of the class because his brain was "addled". You have the Nobel Prize physicist Enrico Fermi, who at 17 had read enough mathematics to qualify for a doctor's degree. And you have the great Albert Schweitzer, who wavered between music and the church until he was 30. Then he started his medical studies.

DARW IN HATED SCHOOL

Charles Darwin's early life was a mess. He hated school, and his father once shouted, "You care for nothing but shooting dogs and rat catching, and you will be a **disgrace**① to yourself and all your family!" He was sent to Glasgow to study medicine, but he couldn't stand the sight of blood. He was sent to divinity school and barely managed to graduate. Whereupon he chucked the whole

① disgrace [dis'greis] n. 丢脸，耻辱；失宠；丢脸的事或人

画——少年时期对音乐不感兴趣的那些人。准确地说，他从未在任何领域表现出超凡的天赋。最终，他选择了法律，但期末考试门门不及格。直到 22 岁那年，他突然对音乐有了强烈的兴趣。他的名字就叫彼得·伊里奇·柴科夫斯基。

爱迪生是“愚蠢”的

在科学领域里，有许多天才在早年时便瞄准了自己的目标，而有的却从未显露过自己的天赋。就是因为这样，我们才有了从小擅长机械引擎的莱特兄弟；有了因为“愚蠢”而差点被老师赶出教室的托马斯·阿尔瓦·爱迪生；有了 17 岁便博览数学类书籍并获得博士学位的诺贝尔物理学奖获得者恩里科·费米；有了 30 岁之前还在音乐和牧师之间犹豫不决，之后才开始学医的伟大的埃博特·施威茨。

达尔文讨厌上学

查尔斯·达尔文早年的生活就像一团乱麻。他讨厌上学。有一次，父亲冲他大声喊道：“除了打狗和追老鼠，你什么都不会。你会成为你自己和家人的耻辱！”就这样，他被送到格拉斯哥学医，可是他一见到血就晕。无奈之下，他又被送到神学院，可是他却无法毕业。于是他抛下一切，乘

business and shipped out to the South Seas on the famous exploring ship Beagle. On that voyage, one of history's greatest scientists was born. It was here that he collected the material for the book that would revolutionize biological science—The Origin of the Species.

FAULKNER FAILED IN ENGLISH

Politics offers a familiar example of contrast. Herbert Hoover must have learned administration in the cradle. When he was at school he was drafted as football manager, though he didn't know the game, and the glee club manager, though he couldn't sing a note. Whatever he touched went smoothly, glee club or food for a starving Europe.

But one of his successors in the White House had about as checkered a youth as can be imagined. Turned down by West Point because of poor vision, Harry Truman tried a dozen jobs, including in a drugstore, a bank, a bottling works, and a railroad yard. But he got there just the same.

Great writers are supposed to be born, not made, but here again there are many fascinating exceptions. William Faulkner quit school in the fifth grade and rattled around the country as a house painter and a dishwasher.

Once he tried attending college, but failed in freshman English and quit. He wangled a postmaster's job in a small Mississippi town, and infuriated the populace by getting the mail all mixed up and closing the office whenever he felt like it. Faulkner was 25 before he started the writing career that won him a Nobel Prize.

坐著名的探险之船——比格——来到南海。历史上最伟大的科学家之一就在此次航海中诞生了。《物种起源》——这本足以引发一场生物科学变革的书，它的素材就是在这次航海中搜集到的。

福克纳英语考试不及格

政界为我们提供了一个熟悉的反例。赫伯特·胡佛一定在婴儿时期便学会了行政管理。在学校，他是校足球队队长，尽管他对足球一窍不通；他也是校合唱队的队长，尽管他对唱歌也是一无所知。凡是他参加的活动总能顺利开展，不论是组织合唱队，还是为欧洲筹集食物。

然而，在白宫，他的一位接班人的青年时代却充满了艰辛。因为视力不佳未被西点军校录取的哈里·杜鲁门试着做过许多工作，包括在药店、银行、装瓶厂和铁路换装场上班。可他终究还是坐上了总统的宝座。

伟大的作家照理说应是天生的，而非后天塑造的。可这儿有许多典型的例外。威廉·福克纳五年级时便辍学了，从此他就穿梭在全国各地，靠给别人油漆房子和洗碗为生。

他曾经上过大学，可在大一的英语考试中，他就考了个不及格，于是他便辍学不上了。他用诈骗手段在密西西比亚的小镇上找到了一份邮递员的工作。可是他把邮件弄得一团糟，令民众激怒不已，并且由着自己的性子想什么时候收工就什么时候收工。在福克纳开始那段给自己带来诺贝尔奖的写作生涯时，他已经 25 岁了。

HOW ABOUT THOSE PRODIGIES

And added to all the aforementioned **paradoxes**[①] you have a small army of child prodigies who were graduated from college when they were 15, and are now obscure clerks in accounting departments. And you have a small army of men who were too stupid or indolent to get into or finish college and who are today presidents of the firms that hire the prodigies.

So who's to say what about youth? Any young boy or girl who knows what he wants to do in life is probably the better off for it. But no teenager needs despair of the future. He has that one special advantage over the greatest man alive—time! If you don't think time counts, look at Grandma Moses, she never sold a painting till she was 80.

① paradox ['pærədɔks] n. 自相矛盾的议论 / 人 / 事

如何解释这些神童呢?

除了前面提到的那些怪才，你也知道不少神童。他们有的 15 岁便大学毕业，可最后却沦为财务部的一名小职员。也有一些孩子，因为当年太笨或太懒而放弃了大学，如今却成了聘请昔日神童的那些公司的总裁。

那么，关于青春，到底谁说了算呢? 任何心中拥有人生目标的少男少女都可能处于优势地位。但任何青少年都无需对未来感到绝望。和一位尚在人间的伟人相比，他拥有一个特别的优势——时间！如果你觉得时间算不上什么，那就请你看看摩西奶奶吧！直到 80 岁她才卖出第一幅画。

From Dreamers to Doers

与其做梦不如行动

◎ Allison Burgess

Most potential entrepreneurs dream of breakthrough businesses all their lives and never get started. On the other hand, those who have listened to their intuition often wish they took the plunge earlier.

When surveyed, **entrepreneurs**① say 29 is the ideal age to start a business. The average age that entrepreneurs actually start a business is 35. They wish they'd started earlier.

There's no perfect age to start living your dreams. Being too young or too old is no excuse. The perfect time to start is right now.

These people did.

Nola Ochs—the Energizer Student

1972. Nola Ochs is widowed on her wheat farm in the town of Jetmore, Kansas (population 1000). She tends to her farm with the help of her children. In 1978, she realizes she wants more from life. Age 68, she signs up for a tennis class at the nearest community college.

Years pass. Nola works full-time on her farm and occasionally drives into town to attend a class. After ten years studying everything from agribusiness to the Bible, she's told that she is one class away from an associate's degree. All she

① entrepreneur [ˌɔntrəprəˈnəː] n. 企业家；事业创办者；承包人

美丽语录

There's never a perfect age to live your dreams. The perfect age is right now.

根本没有所谓的实现梦想的理想年龄。最佳时机就是立刻开始。

世界上很多人都有成为创业家的潜力，可惜他们一生都在蹉跎中度过了，从未实现自己的创业梦想。另一方面，那些听从了直觉的企业家也常常感叹自己没有早点放手一搏。

调查结果显示，企业家们认为 29 岁是创业的理想年龄。然而，企业家真正开始创业的平均年龄却是 35 岁。他们都希望自己能早点开始创业。

其实根本没有所谓的实现梦想的理想年龄。年纪太小或太大都不是理由。最佳时机就是立刻开始。

这些企业家就是这样做的。

诺拉·奥克斯——不安分的学生

1972 年，诺拉·奥克斯独自一人居住在堪萨斯州杰特摩尔镇（人口 1000）一个种植小麦的农场上。她在子女的帮助下照管农场。1978 年，她意识到自己的生活应该是丰富多彩的。68 岁时，她到最邻近的社区大学报名参加了一个网球班。

多年后，诺拉全身心投入到农场上，只是偶尔开车到镇上上课。10 年间，从农业综合业到圣经，她学了一样又一样。拿大专学位的话，她只剩代数一门课程未学完。她要做的就是修完大学代数。

must do is complete college **algebra**[1].

With an associate's degree she is pleased but not fulfilled. College algebra will not be the end of her scholarly career. Several years later she decides to make the two- hour trek to Fort Hays State University. Enrolling at age 94, she lacks only 30 class hours to earn a bachelor's degree. In May 2007, at 95, she becomes the world's oldest college graduate.

Is it time to sit back and enjoy the framed diploma on the farmhouse wall? Not yet. She's started a Masters Degree.

Cliff Burgess—the Marathon Man

1993. Cliff Burgess is 55. He's tired of his potbelly and vows to start walking.

Cliff hits the pavement in his suburban Texas town. A walk around the block turns into twice around the block. Walking feels good, but he knows he can pick up some speed. The weight starts to come off as he signs up for 5km and 10km races. In less than a year, he enters in the San Antonio marathon thinking of it as a training run in preparation for his first marathon—42km (26.2 miles). He feels good during the race, and he crosses the finish line faster than expected.

Averaging 15 **marathons**[2] per year, he completes his 100th marathon six years later at the age of 62.

Reaching 100 marathons isn't the final goal. His running gives him an excuse to travel the world to add to his marathon list. He finds himself in Finland, France, Romania, China, Argentina, Brazil, 25 other countries, and nearly all of the 50 states of the USA in a record 15 years.

---

① algebra ['ældʒibrə] n. 代数学

② marathon ['mærəθɑn] n. 马拉松赛跑；长距离比赛；耐力比赛

获得大专学位，她很高兴，但不满足。学完代数这门课并不意味着她的学涯就此结束。多年后，她决定花两小时开车到富特海斯州立大学上课。入学时，她已经 94 岁了。她还差 30 个课程才能获得学士学位。2007 年的 5 月，95 岁的她成为了世界上最年长的大学毕业生。

她是不是应该坐下欣赏挂在农舍墙上的那张裱起来的文凭呢？还是不行。她又开始攻读硕士学位了。

克里夫·伯吉斯——参加马拉松的老汉

1993 年，克里夫·伯吉斯 55 岁。他厌倦了自己的啤酒肚，于是决定开始散步。

克里夫看上了德州小镇郊外的那条柏油马路。在街区行走一圈慢慢变成了两圈。散步让他觉得很舒服，可他知道自己应该走得更快一些。体重开始减少了，他报名参加了 5 公里和 10 公里的赛跑。不到一年时间，他进入了圣·安东尼奥马拉松队。他把平时跑步当作是自己首次参加马拉松比赛——42 公里（26.2 英里）的赛前训练。比赛时，他感觉良好，冲过终点的速度比他预想的还要快。

他平均每年参加 15 场马拉松比赛。6 年后，62 岁的他跑完了 100 场马拉松赛。

跑完 100 场马拉松赛并非他的终极目标。他的长跑经历让他有了充分的理由，把跑遍全世界列入自己的马拉松计划中。15 年来，他发现自己的马拉松参赛记录遍布芬兰、法国、罗马尼亚、中国、阿尔及利亚、巴西等 25 个国家，还几乎跑遍了了美国 50 个州。

At age 70, he's at Marathon #226 and counting. One of his finest highlights is qualifying multiple times for the runner's dream: a bib number in the Boston Marathon. In April 2009, he will travel to Boston, Massachusetts for the fourth time to take part yet again in all the running glory.

"Nothing happens unless first we dream."

— Carl Sandburg

Action summary

● Make your goal known. Travel one step at a time.

● Keep your dream alive. Long-term goals exist because they take a long time.

● Success and determination are intimate siblings. Talent is merely success's distant cousin.

70 岁时，他总计参加了 226 场马拉松赛。他最引以自豪的一样东西，就是多次取得赛跑者梦寐以求的参赛资格——他拿到了波士顿马拉松赛的参赛选手编号。2009 年 4 月，他将第四次到马萨诸塞州的波士顿参赛，一展自己的长跑辉煌。

“除非我们梦想在先，否则只能一事无成。”

——卡尔・桑德伯格

行动总结

- 明确你的目标，一步一个脚印。
- 让你的梦想永远充满活力。长期的目标需要长时间的努力。
- 成功和决心是最亲的兄弟姐妹。天赋只是成功的远房亲戚。

Young People Should Have Ideals
年轻人应该有理想

© Paul Angone

To different people, the word "ideal" may mean different things. To some, it may mean success and fame in their career; to others, a peaceful life. Very often, we have ideals for the "self" and no ideal for society, not to mention the people of the world. Is it a sound attitude towards life?

In my opinion, a youth should have ideals. But it is more important that these ideals are not merely **centered on**[①] the "self". They should be also the ideals of the majority of people. Then you would get strength and confidence towards life.

The setting up of an ideal does not merely mean to go without doing anything. Real and concrete action should be taken. For us students, the most important thing to do is to study both inside and outside school. We study not to become bookworms but to be **well-equipped**[②] and prepared for the **pursuit**[③] of our ideals.

Sometimes, in striving toward our ideals, we may encounter certain difficulties and failures. But we should not give up or lose hope, for as long as we try, there is always a way out. We will not lose heart if our ideals are the wish of the many!

---

① center on 把……集中在，以……为中心
② well-equipped adj. 设备精良的
③ pursuit [pə'sju:t] n. 追踪，追击

美丽语录

If you identify your way, the world is gonna give way to you.

如果你明确自己的方向，世界也会为你让路。

“理想”一词对于不同的人可能有着不同的含义。在一些人看来，它可能意味着事业上的成功和名誉；而在另一些人看来，它可能意味着平静的生活。一般情况下，我们有为“自我”的理想，却没有为社会的理想，至于为全人类的理想就更不用提了。这是一种健康的人生态度吗?

我认为年轻人应该有理想。然而，更为重要的是，这些理想不能仅仅以“自我”为中心，而应以大多数人的理想为中心。这样，你才能得到力量，并对生活充满信心。

确立一个理想不能夸夸其谈，而应该采取真正的、具体的行动。对于我们学生来说，最重要的事不仅是在校内学习，还要在校外学习。我们学习的目的不是为了学成书呆子，而是为了好好地武装自己，为了作好准备去追求我们的理想。

有时，在向着理想前进的时候，我们可能会经历一些困难和失败。然而，我们不应该放弃或丧失希望，因为只要我们尝试了，终究会有摆脱困境的办法。假如我们的理想正是许多人的愿望，我们就不会丧失勇气！

A Time to Awake
觉醒时分

◎ Dawn

What has become of your fondest dreams? If you were **guaranteed**① success, what would you dare to attempt?

We all have dreams, deep inside... Those moments when we take a voyage in our imagination, into a world where everything was possible, a world where fear is a strange concept, limits are non-existent and we are at peace with ourselves.

How come our dreams remain just those dreams? Why are we stuck in jobs we hate, held bound by the fear of the unknown, if we dare to stand up and walk away?

Every new day seems to take us farther away from our dream. Sometimes we get so caught up in the rat race; our dreams seem like a distant memory. Little by little we let our dreams die.

How come our biggest dreams don't come true? The answer is not a profound revelation from the east, culled from wisdom of the ancients. It is so simple, you begin to wonder why it skipped you all these years.

---

① guaranteed [ˈgærənˈtiːd] adj. 必定的，肯定的

美丽语录

Re a long way, a step by step can be completed, and then a short road, do not stride feet cannot be reached.

再长的路，一步步也能走完；再短的路，不迈开双脚也无法到达。

你最渴望的梦想怎么样了？如果你注定会成功，那么你还敢尝试些什么呢？

我们都有梦想，深深地埋藏在心里……带着梦想，我们乘着想象之翼，进入一个一切皆有可能的世界。那是一个没有恐惧、没有限制、人人心境宁静的世界。

为何我们的梦想依旧只是梦想呢？假如我们勇敢地站起来走开，那我们是不是就不会陷入厌恶的工作中，被莫名其妙的恐惧困扰呢？

每个崭新的一天都好像让我们离梦想越来越远。有时，我们被毫无意义的竞争困扰着；有时，我们的梦想就像是一段遥不可及的回忆。渐渐地，我们的梦想幻灭了。

为何我们最大的梦想无法实现？答案并不是从东方古人的智慧中领悟出的深刻启迪。它其实十分简单，你甚至会开始思考，为什么这么多年自己却都没有发现。

Our dreams simply don't come true because we keep on sleeping after dreaming. We don't wake up, get out of bed, and do something about it. The best dreams come to pass when you are awake.

Sometimes we actually wake up and take one giant leap for mankind. Then we **plummet**[①] back to earth, lick our wounds, and convince ourselves that it is not feasible and promptly go back to sleep. Sometimes we give it a second or third shot, before we say goodbye and return to Status Quo Avenue. Well, we gave our best shot...

The only way our dreams can come true is when we start doing something about it. Start with a baby step, one tiny step after another. With time, you will be amazed by how far you had gone. The more steps you take in the direction of your dreams, the bolder you become. Soon you start seeing shafts of light at the end of the tunnel. The closer you get, the more feasible it becomes. Gradually, your fears begin to ebb away. Taking the first step is a scary business. You can determine the **magnitude**[②] and direction of that first step. Some folks take the bull by the horn, quit their day jobs, and go for it. Others keep their day jobs, and moonlight at sun down, till they get to the point they can comfortably fire their boss. For others still, it means a change of career.

Whichever route you take to the land of your dreams, the starting point is waking up, and doing something. Then keep on keeping on. It is only a matter of time. You will get there.

---

① plummet ['plʌmit] n. 坠子，测铅；重压
② magnitude ['mægnitju:d] n. 巨大，广大；大小

我们的梦想无法实现的原因其实很简单，那就是：我们做完梦便又再次沉沉地睡着了。我们没有立刻醒来，起床，然后将它实现。等你醒来时，最好的梦想都已消失不见。

有时，我们的确醒来了，还为全人类的进步迈出了一大步。接着，我们便摔倒在地，只顾舔舐伤口，劝自己说这是不可行的，不一会儿便又回到了梦乡。有时，在彻底放弃和安于现状之前，我们会象征性地尝试一两次。那么，我们真的尽力了吗?

让梦想实现的唯一方法就是：动起来。先迈一小步，接着再迈一小步。随着时间的推移，你会惊奇地发现自己已经走了很远。你朝着梦想的方向迈的步子越多，你就会越勇敢。很快，你就能看见隧道另一端的光亮了。你越靠近它，就越可能实现梦想。慢慢地，你的恐惧消失不见了。迈出第一步是一件让人恐慌的事情。但是，第一步的大小和方向全都掌握在你的手中。有些人勇敢地面对困难，辞去工作，去追逐梦想；而另一些人则选择留在原地，继续着从前那起早贪黑的日子，直到自己也有勇气炒老板鱿鱼的那一天。毕竟对这些人来说，这意味着要转变职业道路。

无论你选择以哪种方式实现自己的梦想，起点永远都是：醒过来，动起来，然后继续下去。能否实现梦想，这只是时间问题。你终将到达目的地。

The Strenuous Life
艰辛的人生

◎ Theodore Roosevelt

A life of slothful ease, a life of that peace which springs merely from lack either of desire or of power to strive after great things, is as little worthy of a nation as an individual.

We do not admire the man of timid peace. We admire the man who embodies victorious efforts, the man who never wrongs his neighbor, who is prompt to help a friend, but who has those virile qualities necessary to win in the **stern**[①] strife of actual life. It is hard to fail, but it is worse never to have tried to succeed. In this life we get nothing save by effort. Freedom from effort in the present merely means that there has been effort stored up in the past. A man can be free from the necessity of work only by the fact that he or his fathers before him have worked to good purpose. If the freedom thus purchased is used aright, and the man still does actual work, though of a different kind, whether as a writer or a general, whether in the field of politics or in the field of exploration and adventure, he shows he deserves his good fortune.

But if he treats this period of freedom from the need of actual labor as a

① stern [stəːn] adj. 严峻的，苛刻的；不动摇的

美丽语录

Miracles sometimes occur, but you have to work terribly for them.

奇迹有时候是会发生的，但是你得为之拼命努力。

一种慵懒安逸的生活，一种仅仅是因为缺少追寻伟大事物的渴望或能力而引起的悠闲，这样的个人对国家来说是毫无价值的。

我们不会羡慕那些怯懦安逸的人。我们只会欣赏那种奋力向上的人；那种永不错怪邻里，乐于帮助朋友，而且很有男子气概，能够战胜现实生活的残酷竞争的人。失败是痛苦的，可从来没为成功放手一搏则更糟糕。在人的一生中，任何收获都是通过努力得到的。现在不用努力，只是意味着过去积攒的努力尚有余留。一个人不必工作，除非他或他的祖先曾经努力工作过，并取得了丰厚的收获。如果他能利用换取到的自由做些实际的工作，尽管那是一份不同的工作，不论是成为作家或将军，不论是在政治领域或是探险和冒险方面，都表明他值得拥有这份财富。

然而，如果在这段不用工作的时间里，他不知“未雨绸缪”，只知享乐（尽管他所从事的或许并非邪恶的享乐），那就表明了他只是地球表面上的

period, not of preparation, but of mere enjoyment, even though perhaps not of vicious enjoyment, he shows that he is simply a cumberer on the earth's surface; and he surely unfits himself to hold his own place with his fellows, if the need to do so should again arise. A mere life of ease is not in the end a very satisfactory life, and, above all, it is a life which ultimately unfits those who follow it for serious work in the world.

As it is with the individual, so it is with the nation. It is a base untruth to say that happy is the nation that has no history. Thrice happy is the nation that has a glorious history. Far better it is to dare mighty things, to win glorious **triumphs**[①], even though checkered by failure, than to take rank with those poor spirits who neither enjoy much nor suffer much, because they live in the gray twilight that knows neither victory nor defeat.

① triumph ['traiəmf] n.（大）胜利；成功，业绩

一个赘疣。当他再次需要在伙伴面前维持自己昔日的地位时，他就注定会失败。安逸的生活终究不会是令人满意的生活。更重要的是，过着安逸生活的那些人，肯定无力担当世间的重任。

这对国家和个人来说，都是一样的。没有历史的国家是一个幸福的国度，这简直就是最可耻的谎言。拥有光辉历史的国家才是最幸福的国度。为了伟大事业而身陷险境，为了赢得光荣胜利而吃尽失败之苦，那也胜过与没有享受过多大快乐、也没有遭受过多大苦的平庸之人为伍（因为他们生活在一个个既享受不到胜利，也遭遇不到失败的灰暗世界里）。

Universities and Their Function

大学的意义

◎ Alfred North Whitehead

The justification for a university is that it preserves the connection between knowledge and the zest of life, by uniting the young and the old in the imaginative consideration of learning. The university imparts information, but it imparts it imaginatively. At least, this is the function which it should perform for society. A university which fails in this respect has no reason for existence. This atmosphere of excitement, arising from imaginative consideration, transforms knowledge. A fact is no longer a bare fact: it is invested with all its possibilities. It is no longer a burden on the memory: it is energizing as the poet of our dreams, and as the **architect**① of our purposes.

Imagination is not to be divorced from the facts: it is a way of **illuminating**② the facts. It works by drawing the general principles which apply to the facts, as they exist, and then by an intellectual survey of alternative possibilities which are consistent with those principles. It enables men to construct an intellectual vision of a new world, and it preserves the zest of life by the suggestion of satisfying purposes.

① architect ['akitekt] n. 建筑师，设计师；缔造者，创造者
② illuminate [i'lju:mineit] v. 照亮，照射；启发

美丽语录

A soul without imagination is like an observatory without the telescope.

没有想象力的灵魂，就像没有望远镜的天文台。

大学存在的理由在于它让新老两代人在想象中学习，从而让知识和生活的热情连结起来。大学是传授知识的，但它是以一种富有想象力的方式进行传授。至少，这是它应该为社会发挥的作用。一所大学若连这点都无法做到，那它就毫无存在的理由。一个富于想象的人很容易感到兴奋激动，从而使知识得以彻底转化。事实也远非事实本身，它具有了所有潜在的可能。它不再是记忆的负担，而是像描绘我们美梦的诗人和实现我们心愿的设计师那样充满活力。

想象与事实不可分离：是它让事实变得鲜明。它让人们获得与存在的事实相一致的一般原则，让人们能够理性地审视那些和一般原则相一致的各种可能性。它让人们构建出一个关于新世界的理性视觉。它用一些令人满意的方法让生活的激情得以持续。

Youth is imaginative, and if the imagination be strengthened by discipline this energy of imagination can in great measure be preserved through life. The tragedy of the world is that those who are imaginative have but slight experience, and those who are experienced have **feeble**[①] imaginations. Fools act on imagination without knowledge; pedants act on knowledge without imagination. The task of a university is to weld together imagination and experience.

① feeble [fi:bl] adj. 虚弱无力的；拙劣无效的；站不住脚的

青年是富有想象力的。假使加强想象的训练，那么它就能在生活中得以完好地保存。这个世界的悲剧在于：那些富有想象力的人却经验不足，而那些富有经验的人却缺乏想象。没有知识的傻瓜全凭想象办事，没有想象力的书呆子则只凭知识办事。大学的任务就是让想象和经验结合在一起。

The Shoe Tacks

鞋钉

© Tom Cawley

The hardworking blacksmith Jones used to work all day in his shop and so hard working was he that at times he would make the sparks fly from his hammer. The son of Mr. Smith, a rich neighbor, used to come to see the blacksmith everyday and for hours and hours he would enjoy himself watching how the **tradesman**[1] worked.

"Young man, why don't you try your hand to learn to make shoe tacks, even if it is only to pass the time?" said the blacksmith. "Who knows, one day, it may be of use to you." The lazy boy began to see what he could do. But after a little practice he found that he was becoming very skilled and soon he was making some of the finest tacks.

Old Mr. Smith died and the son on account of the war lost all his goods. He had to leave home and was forced to take up residence in another country. It so happened that in this village there were **numerous**[2] shoemakers who were spending a lot of money to buy tacks for their shoes and even at times when they

① tradesman [treidzmən] n. 零售商，店主；手艺人，技工
② numerous ['nju:mərəs] adj. 许多的；为数众多的

美丽语录

Give everything a shot. You never know what (or who) is going to change your life.

任何事情都应该去尝试一下，因为你无法知道，什么样的事或人将会改变你的一生。

琼斯是个勤劳的铁匠，常常一整天都在他的店里工作。他工作非常努力，他的锤子时常会火花四溅。史密斯先生的儿子，一个很有钱的邻居，几乎每天都来看铁匠工作。他喜欢观看这位工匠工作，而且一看就是几小时。

“年轻人，你为什么不尝试一下如何制作鞋钉呢，哪怕只是用来消磨时间？”铁匠说，“谁知道呢，有一天，它或许就会对你有用呢。”那个懒孩子开始想看看自己到底能做什么。但是，仅仅经过小小的实践练习，他就发现自己变得非常熟练，很快他就做出了最好的鞋钉。

老史密斯先生去世了，他的儿子则因为战争而失去了所有的财产。他不得不离开家园，被迫住在了另一个国家。事情就是这样巧合，这个国家的这个地区急需大量军鞋，所以这个村子里有很多鞋匠，而他们总是花费

paid high prices they were not always able to get what they wanted, because in that part of the country there was a high demand for soldiers' shoes.

Our young Mr. Smith, who was finding it difficult to earn his daily bread, remembered that once upon a time he had learned the art of making tacks and had the sudden idea of making a **bargain**[①] with the shoemakers. He told them that he would make the tacks if they would help to get him settled in his workshop. The shoemakers were only too glad of the offer. And after a while, Mr. Smith found that he was soon making the finest tacks in the village. "How funny it seems," he used to say, "Even making tacks can bring a fortune. My trade is more useful to me than were all my former riches."

① bargain ['bɑ:gin] n. 协议；买卖，交易

很多钱购买鞋钉。甚至有时即使付了很高的价钱，也买不到他们想要的鞋钉。

在这食不果腹的艰难时刻，我们的小史密斯先生想起了自己从前学过制鞋钉这门手艺，突然冒出了一个想法，和这些鞋匠们做一个交易。他告诉他们，如果他们帮他成立一个店铺，他就可以做鞋钉。结果，鞋匠们对他的这一提议欣喜若狂。过了不久，史密斯先生发现他做的鞋钉是村里最好的。“看起来可真有意思，”他常常会说，“即便是做鞋钉也会带来财富。与我以前所有的财富相比，我现在的生意更有益。”

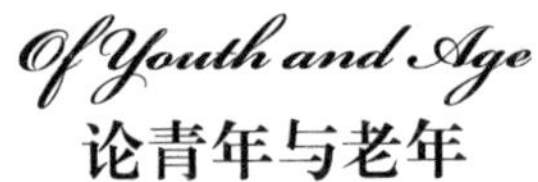

论青年与老年

◎ Francis Bacon

A man that is young in years may be old in hours, if he has lost no time. But that happened rarely. Generally, youth is like the first **cogitating**[①], not so wise as the second. For there is a youth in thoughts, as well as in ages.

And yet the invention of young men is more lively than that of old; and imaginations stream into their minds better, and, as it were, more divinely. Natures that have much heat, and great and violent desires and **perturbations**[②], are not ripe for action, till they have passed the meridian of their years; as it was with Julius Caesar and Septimius Severus...

Young men are fitter to invent, than to judge; fitter for execution, than for counsel; and fitter for new projects, than for settled business, for the experience of age, in things that fall within the compass of it, directeth them; but in new things, abuseth them.

The errors of young men, are the ruin of business; but the errors of aged men, amount but to this, that more might have been done, or sooner, Young men,

① cogitate ['kɔdʒiteit] v. 仔细考虑；谋划

② perturbation [ˌpəːtə'beiʃən] n. 扰乱，混乱；烦恼

美丽语录

Learn from yesterday, live for today, hope for tomorrow.

学习昨天，活在今天，期待明天。

一个岁数不大的年轻人也能表现得十分老练，只要他不曾虚度光阴。但这毕竟是少有的事。一般而言，青年的“初念”不如老年的“深思”明智。即使是年纪相仿的青年人，他们的区别关乎年龄，也关乎思想。

然而，青年的发明相比老年要来得有活力，就连想象力也如泉涌，犹如神助那般。生性热切、欲望满满、忧虑不安的青年必须历经中年，才能成熟处事，凯撒和塞维拉就是最好的例子……

青年擅长创造，却不懂判断，擅长执行却不懂商酌，擅长革新却不懂借鉴经验。日积月累的经验就像指南针，引领青年掌握旧事物，却也蒙蔽了用来发现新事物的双眼。

青年人犯的错，通常会影响大局。可老年人犯的错，最多只是力气太小或行动迟缓。青年人在行为及其管理上，总是好大喜功，行事高调，好走极端，欠缺方式和分寸上的考虑；他们只知追循偶然发现的前例，却无

in the conduct and manage of actions, embrace more than they can hold; stir more than they can quiet; fly to the end, without consideration of the means and degrees; pursue some few principles, which they have chanced upon absurdly care not to innovate, which draws unknown inconveniences; use extreme remedies at first; and, that which doubleth all errors, will not acknowledge or retract them; like and unready horse; that will neither stop nor turn. Men of age object too much, consult too long adventure too little, repent too soon, and seldom drive business home to the full period, but content themselves with a **mediocrity**??① of success. Certainly it is good to compound employments of both; and good for succession, that young men may be learners, while men in age are actors; and, lastly, good for extern accidents, because authority followeth old men, and favor and popularity, youth. But for the moral part, perhaps youth will have the pre-eminence, as age hath for the politic.

① mediocrity [ˌmi:di'ɔkriti] n. 平凡；平庸的人

心改革，因而招致一些不必要的麻烦。他们行事极端，却不思补救，最后只会一错再错，就如脱缰的野马，停不下来更无法回头。至于老年人，他们顾虑太多，商量太久，经常懊悔，却又不敢冒险。他们宁可安于平凡也不愿追求超凡。当然，如果能将这两者的特点相结合，那是最好不过了。在长远发展方面，老年人可以是行动者，而青年人则是学习者；在外来压力方面，老年人是权威的代表，而青年人则深受欢迎和喜爱；在道德方面，老年人和青年人都能成为杰出的政治人物。

走向最美的旅行

In life, there is no station, no one place to arrive at once and for all. The true joy of life is the trip. The station is only a dream.

人生的旅途中并没有车站，也没有一个一劳永逸的地方。生活的真正乐趣在于旅行的过程，而车站只是一个梦。

Feed Your Mind

充实你的思想

◎ Deepak Chandrase karan

Since the pre-historic times, man has had an urge to satisfy his needs. Be it hunger, shelter or search for a mate, he has always **manipulated**[①] the circumstances to the best of his advantages. Probably this might be the reason why we human are the most developed of all living species on the earth, and probably also in the universe. As we climbed the steps of evolution with giant leaps, we somehow left behind common sense and logical thinking—we forgot that we have stopped thinking ahead of times.

If you are hungry, what do you do? Grab a piece of your favorite meal and stay quiet after that? Just like your stomach, even your mind is hungry. But it never lets you know, because you keep it busy thinking about your dream lover, favorite star and many such absurd things. So it silently began to heed to your needs and never let itself grow. When mind looses its freedom to grow, creativity gets a full stop. This might be the reason why we all sometimes think "What happens next?", "Why can't I think?", "Why am I always given the difficult

① manipulate [mə'nipjuleit] v.（熟练地）操作，运用；巧妙处理

美丽语录

You can either travel or read, and either your body or soul must be on the way.

要么旅行，要么读书，身体和灵魂，必须有一个在路上。

自史前时代起，人类就已有满足自己需求的强烈欲望。无论是饥饿、避难或寻觅配偶，人类总是操纵着环境使其达到最利于自己的状态。这或许解答了为什么我们人类是地球上甚至是宇宙中最发达的现存物种。然而在进化的阶梯上取得巨大飞跃之时，我们却不知何故将一些常识和逻辑思维抛诸脑后了——我们忘记了自己已经停止了超前思维。

如果你饿了，你会怎么做？抓起你最喜爱的美食饱餐一顿，然后静静呆在那里？就像你的胃一样，你的大脑也会感到饥饿。但它却从不让你知道，因为你让它一直忙着想你的梦中情人、你最喜爱的明星和许多荒谬的事情。所以，它只是静静地留意着你的需求，却从不让它自己成长。当思维恣意成长时，创造力会就此画上句号。这也许就是为什么我们有时会想“接下来该如何？”“为什么我想不到？”“为什么我总是碰到难题？”的原

problems?" Well this is the **aftermath**[1] of our own karma of using our brain for thinking of not-so-worthy things.

Hunger of the mind can be actually satiated through extensive reading. Now why reading and not watching TV? Because reading has been the most educative tool used by us right from the childhood. Just like that to develop other aspects of our life, we have to take help of reading. You have innumerable number of books in this world which will answer all your "How to?" questions. Once you read a book, you just don't run your eyes through the lines, but even your mind decodes it and explains it to you. The interesting part of the book is stored in your mind as a seed. Now this seed is unknowingly used by you in your future to develop new ideas. The same seed if used many times can help you link and relate a lot of things, of which you would have never thought of in your wildest dreams! This is nothing but creativity. More the number of books you read, your mind will open up like never before. Also this improves your oratory skills to a large extent and also makes a significant contribution to your vocabulary. Within no time you start speaking English or any language fluently with your friends or other people and you never seem to run out of the right words at the right time.

Actually, I had a problem in speaking English fluently, but as I read, I could improve significantly. I am still on the path of improvement to **quench**[2] my thirst for satisfaction. So guys do join me and give food for your thoughts by reading, reading and more reading. Now what are you waiting for? Go, grab a book, and let me know!

---

① aftermath ['ɑ:ftəmæθ] n. 后果，余波；事件结束后的一段时期

② quench [kwentʃ] v. 压制（欲望等），抑制；熄灭；平息

因吧。对了，这也是我们的大脑总在考虑那些毫无价值的事情所产生的后果。

事实上，思维的饥荒可以通过广泛的阅读得到满足。那么，为什么是阅读而不是看电视呢？因为自孩提时代起，阅读就已经是最具教育性的工具了。正如人生发展的其他方面一样，我们不得不求助于阅读。世界上有无数的书籍可以回答你“如何做”的问题。读书时，不仅只是让你的眼睛扫过文字，还要用你的脑子去解读、诠释。书中有趣的部分就会像种子一样贮存在你的脑海里。将来你会不自觉地运用这粒种子引发新的思路。多次运用这粒种子，这将有助于你把许多事情联系起来，即使你连做最夸张的梦都想不到这些！这不是别的，就是创造力！你读的书越多，你的头脑就会前所未有的开阔。这也在很大程度上提高了你的演讲水平，极大地丰富了你的词汇量。你很快就能用流利的英语或其他语言与你的朋友或其他人交谈，而且你再也不会在合适的时间缺少合适的词语。

事实上，我的英语还是不够流利，但只要我阅读，我就可以大大改善。现在我仍在“自我提高”、为头脑“解渴”的长路上跋涉。加入我的行列吧！通过阅读、阅读、再阅读来为你的思想“喂食”。现在，你还在犹豫什么呢？去，拿起一本书，让我瞧瞧！

The Two Roads

两条路

◎ John Ruskin

It was New Year's Night. An aged man was standing at a window. He raised his mournful eyes towards the deep blue sky, where the stars were floating like white lilies on the surface of a clear calm lake. Then he cast them on the earth, where few more hopeless people than himself now moved towards their certain goal—the **tomb**[①]. He had already passed sixty of the stages leading to it, and he had brought from his journey nothing but errors and remorse. Now his health was poor, his mind vacant, his heart sorrowful, and his old age short of comforts.

He looked towards the sky and cried painfully, "O youth, return! O my father, place me once more at the entrance to life, and I'll choose the better way!" But both his father and the days of his youth had passed away.

The days of his youth appeared like dreams before him, and he recalled the serious moment when his father placed him at the entrance of the two roads—one leading to a peaceful, sunny place, covered with flowers, fruits and resounding with soft, sweet songs; the other leading to a deep, dark cave, which was endless, where poison flowed instead of water and where devils and poisonous snakes

① tomb [tu:m] n. 墓；葬身之地；死亡

美丽语录

Life's greatest regret, than the wrong insist, and easily give up.

人生最大的遗憾，莫过于错误的坚持，和轻易的放弃。

那是一个新年夜。一位老人站在窗前，他那忧伤的双眼眺望着深远蔚蓝的天空。繁星就像是漂浮在平静、清澈湖面上的朵朵白百合。接着他的目光投向地面，此刻，没有人比他更绝望，因为他正一步步迈向自己的最终归宿——坟墓。他已经走过通向坟墓的六十级台阶，除了过错和悔恨，他什么都没有得到。如今，他体弱多病，精神空虚，心情沮丧，人到晚年无所慰藉。

他仰望星空，痛苦地大声喊道："噢，回来吧，青春！噢，父亲，请再次把我带到人生的岔路口吧！我会选择一条更好的道路！"然而，他的父亲和他的青春一起消逝不见了。

青春的日子如梦一般出现在他眼前。老人想起了父亲将他带到人生岔路口的庄严时刻——一条路通往宁静的、阳光明媚的世界，那里满是鲜花和水果，还有甜美轻柔的歌声回荡在空中；另一条路通往一个深沉、黑暗、看不到尽头的洞穴，那里流淌着的不是水，而是毒液，毒蛇一边爬一边发出嘶嘶声。

他看见黑暗中掠过缕缕亮光，就像是自己挥霍掉的往昔。他看见一颗星星从天边陨落，消失不见，那就是他的化身。他的悔恨，就像是一把利箭，深深地刺进他的心脏。于是，他想起了和自己一同迈入人生的儿时好友。可是，他们找到了通往成功的道路。在这个新年夜，他们备受尊敬，

hissed and crawled.

He saw the lights flowing away in the darkness. These were the days of his wasted life; he saw a star fall from the sky and disappeared, and this was the symbol of himself. His remorse, which was like a sharp arrow, struck deeply into his heart. Then he remembered his friends in his childhood, who entered on life together with him. But they had made their way to success and were now honored and happy on this New Year's night.

The clock in the high church tower struck and the sound made him remember his parents' early love for him. They had taught him and prayed to God for his good. But he chose the wrong way. With shame and grief he dared no longer look towards that heaven where his father live. His darkened eyes were full of tears, and with a **despairing**[①] effort, he burst out a cry: "Come back, my early days! Come back!" And his youth did return, for all this was only a dream which he had on New Year's Night. He was still young though his faults were real; he had not yet entered the deep, dark cave, and he was still free to walk on the road which leads to the peaceful and sunny land.

Those who still **linger**[②] on the entrance of life, hesitating to choose the bright road, remember that when years are passed and your feet stumble on the dark mountains, you will cry bitterly, but in vain: "O youth, return! Oh give me back my early days!"

① despairing [di'spɛəriŋ] adj. 感到绝望的；表现绝望的
② linger ['liŋgə] v. 徘徊；缓慢消失；磨蹭；苟延残喘

幸福无比。

高高的教堂钟楼上传来了钟声，这声音让他回想起父母早年对他的疼爱。他们教育他，祈求上帝保佑他。可是，他选择了一条错误的路。羞愧和悲伤让他不敢仰望父亲所在的天堂。他那双黯淡的双眼噙满了泪水，他绝望地嘶喊道："回来吧！我的往昔！回来吧！"

他的青春真的回来了，所有的这一切只是一个梦，一个在新年夜所做的梦。他依旧年轻，虽然他犯的错是真实存在的；他也没有走进那个深幽、黑暗的洞穴；他依旧可以自由行走在那条通往宁静的、阳光明媚的世界的道路上。

那些仍旧徘徊在人生岔路口，犹豫着该不该选择光明之路的人们，请你们记住，当青春不再，你的双脚跌绊在黑暗的山间时，你会痛苦地呼喊着："噢，青春，回来吧！把我的往昔还给我！"但这一切已是徒然。

On the Feeling of Immortality in Youth
有感于青春常在

◎ William Hazilitt

No young man believes he will ever die. It was a saying of my brother's, and a fine one.

There is a feeling of eternity in youth, which makes us amend for everything.

To be young is to be as one of the immortal Gods.

One half of time indeed is flown—the other half remains in store for us with all its countless treasures, for there is no line drawn, and we see no limit to our hopes and wishes.

We make the coming age our own—the vast, the **unbounded**① prospect lies before us.

Death, old age is words without a meaning that pass by us like the idea air which we regard not.

Others may have undergone, or may still be liable to them—we "bear a charmed life", which laughs to scorn all such sickly fancies. As in setting out on

① unbounded [ʌn'baundid] adj. 无限的；无节制的；不受控制的

美丽语录

Don't let the sadness of your past and the fear of your future ruin the happiness of your present.

别让过去的悲催和未来的忧虑，毁掉自己当下的快乐。

年轻人不相信自己会死。这是我哥哥说的一句话，也算得上一句金玉良言。

青春有种永生之感，它能弥补一切。

永葆年轻就像是成为一尊不朽的神明。

诚然，生命的一半已然消逝——而保留下的另一半将给我们带来无尽的财富，对此我们怀着无限的希望和企盼。

未来的日子掌握在我们自己手中——眼前展现一片无限辽阔的前景。

死亡，衰老，这些毫无意义的字眼，我们只当耳旁风那样听过便忘了。

这一切，也许其他人早已经历，亦或正在承受——我们的生活备受祝福，所以面对这些脆弱的想法，只需一笑置之。就像踏上一段愉快的旅程，我们极目远眺——向着远处的美景欢呼。

前进的路上，看见的是无限的山水美景和不断涌现的新目标。

delightful journey, we strain our eager gaze forward—bidding the lovely scenes at distance hail!

And see no end to the landscape, new objects presenting themselves as we advance.

So, in the commencement of life, we set no bounds to our inclinations, nor to the unrestricted opportunities of gratifying them.

We have as yet found no obstacle, no disposition to flag; and it seems that we can go on so forever.

We look round in a new world, full of life, and motion, and ceaseless progress; and feel in ourselves all the vigor and spirit to keep pace with it, and do not foresee from any present symptoms how we shall be left behind in the natural course of things, decline into old age, and drop into the grave.

It is the simplicity, and as it were abstractedness of our feelings in youth, that identifies us with nature, and deludes us into a belief of being immortal like it.

Our short lives connexion with existence we fondly flatter ourselves is an indissoluble and lasting union—a honeymoon that knows neither coldness, jar, nor separation.

As infants smile and sleep, we are rocked in the cradle of our wayward fancies, and lulled into security by the roar of the universe around us—we **quaff**① the cup of life with eager haste without draining it, instead of which it only overflows the more objects press around us, filling the mind with their magnitude and with the strong of desires that wait upon them, so that we have no room for the thoughts of death.

① quaff [kwa:f] v. 狂饮，痛饮

因此，生命伊始，让我们的志趣自由驰骋，自由寻求一切满足的机会。

然而，我们未曾碰上障碍，也未曾感到疲惫。看样子我们可以永远前进，直到永远。

我们环视这个崭新的世界——生机盎然、日新月异、进取不断。我们深感自己活力四射、精神奕奕，可以跟上宇宙的脚步。眼前也没有迹象表明，在大自然的发展过程中，我们会落伍，会老去，会死去。

年轻时单纯率真，也就是天真无知，让我们误以为自己与大自然无异，并相信自己能和它一样永恒不朽。

我们一厢情愿地把自己在世上的短暂停留当作永恒不变、千古永存的结合——就像没有冷淡、争执和离别的蜜月。

我们就躺在自己用幻想编织而成的摇篮里，像婴儿那般微笑入睡。世间万物发出的声音就像是催眠曲般哄着我们安然入眠。我们渴望地、急切地饮着生命之杯里的美酒，可杯中的美酒怎么也喝不干，反而永远那样满满欲溢。森罗万象和种种欲望占据了一切，就连死亡我们都无暇去想。

Enthusiasm Takes You Further
热情带你前进

◎ Marcus Sheridan

Years ago, when I started looking for my first job, wise advisers urged, "Barbara, be enthusiastic! Enthusiasm will take you further than any amount of experience."

How right they were. Enthusiastic people can turn a boring drive into an adventure, extra work into opportunity and strangers into friends.

"Nothing great was ever achieved without enthusiasm," wrote Ralph Waldo Emerson. It is the **paste**① that helps you hang in there when the going gets tough. It is the inner voice that whispers, "I can do it!" when others shout, "No, you can't."

It took years and years for the early work of Barbara McClintock, a geneticist who won the 1983 Nobel Prize in medicine, to be generally accepted. Yet she didn't let up on her experiments. Work was such a deep pleasure for her that she never thought of stopping.

We are all born with wide-eyed, enthusiastic wonder as anyone knows who has ever seen an infant's delight at the jingle of keys or the scurrying of a beetle.

It is this childlike wonder that gives enthusiastic people such a youthful air, whatever their age.

① paste [peist] n. 浆糊，面团，糊状物

美丽语录

Enjoy the little things in life, for one day you may look back and realize they were the big things.

享受生命中的每一个细节，因为当你回首往事时可能会发现，原来那些所谓的小事是多么的重要。

多年前，当我开始寻找我的第一份工作时，我聪明的指导员敦促我：“芭芭拉，一定要充满热情！热情带给你的东西将远远胜过任何经验带给你的。”

他说得很对。热情似火的人们能把无趣的事情变成一次冒险，把额外的工作变成机会，把陌生人变成好朋友。

“没有热情，再伟大的事情也无法完成。”拉尔夫·瓦尔多·爱默生这样写道。当事情变得棘手时，是浆糊般的韧劲让你坚持下来；当别人冲你高声喊着“不，你做不到”时，是你内心的声音轻声对你说：“我能做到。”

这就是遗传学家芭芭拉·麦克林托克——1983年诺贝尔医学奖的获得者——早年所从事的工作，她花了好几年的时间才使大家普遍接受这个事实。至今，她仍旧一心扑在实验上。对她来说，工作就是一种深入内心的享受。因此，她从未想过要停止工作。

我们生来就有一双大眼睛，天性激情似火。任何一个见过婴儿听到钥匙声或看见乱爬的甲虫就兴奋不已的人，都会明白这一点。

正是这种孩子般的好奇心，让热情似火的人们（不论何种年龄）有一种青春的气息。

At 90, cellist Pablo Casals would start his day by playing Bach. As the music flowed through his fingers, his stooped shoulders would straighten and joy would reappear in his eyes. Music, for Casals, was an **elixir**[1] that made life a never ending adventure. As author and poet Samuel Ullman once wrote, "Years wrinkle the skin, but to give up enthusiasm wrinkles the soul."

How do you rediscover the enthusiasm of your childhood? The answer, I believe, lies in the word itself. "Enthusiasm" comes from the Greek and means "God within." And what is God within is but an abiding sense of love—proper love of self (self-acceptance) and, from that, love of others.

Enthusiastic people also love what they do, regardless of money or title or power. If we cannot do what we love as a full-time career, we can as a part-time avocation, like the head of state who paints, the nun who runs marathons, the executive who handcrafts furniture.

Elizabeth Layton of Wellsville, Kan, was 68 before she began to draw. This activity ended bouts of depression that had plagued her for at least 30 years, and the quality of her work led one critic to say, "I am tempted to call Layton a genius." Elizabeth has rediscovered her enthusiasm.

We can't afford to waste tears on "might-have-beens."We need to turn the tears into sweat as we go after "What-can-be."

We need to live each moment wholeheartedly, with all our senses—finding pleasure in the fragrance of a back-yard garden, the crayoned picture of a six-year-old, the enchanting beauty of a rainbow. It is such enthusiastic love of life that puts a sparkle in our eyes, a lilt in our steps and smooths the wrinkles from our souls.

① elixir n. 炼金药，不老长寿药；万能药

大提琴演奏家帕布罗·卡萨尔斯 90 岁时还坚持以演奏巴赫开始他一天的生活。音乐从他的指尖流出，他弯着的背都挺直了，欢乐再一次溢满他的双眼。对卡萨尔斯来说，音乐是让人生变成一次无止尽的冒险的灵丹妙药。就像作家兼诗人塞缪尔·厄尔曼曾经写道："悠悠岁月，老去的只是容颜；抛弃激情，衰败的就是灵魂！"

你怎样才能重拾孩提时的那份热情呢？我相信答案就在于"热情"这个词本身。"热情"一词源于希腊，它的原意是"内心的上帝"。"内心的上帝"其实不是别的，就是一种亘古不变的爱——适度地爱自己（自我接纳）以及缘于此的爱别人。

热情似火的人同样深爱着他们所做的事，而不会考虑金钱、地位和权力。如果我们不能将自己所钟爱的事情作为自己的正式职业，那么我们可以把它当作业余爱好，就像爱好画画的国家元首，参加马拉松比赛的修女和自己亲手制作家具的行政官员。

堪萨斯州韦尔斯维尔市的伊丽莎白·莱顿 68 岁时才开始画画。这个爱好消除了纠缠她长达 30 年之久的忧郁症，而她的作品也因画技精湛而深获一位评论家的好评："我忍不住要称莱顿为天才。"伊丽莎白又找回了她的热情。

我们不该把眼泪浪费在"早该……"这类忏悔上。我们应该把眼泪化为汗水，去追寻"可能"的东西。

我们应该全心全意地度过生命中的每一分钟——在后花园的芬芳中，在 6 岁小孩的蜡笔画中，在彩虹迷人的美中寻找快乐，打开所有的感知，这才是对生活的热爱。正是这种热爱让我们双目有神，让我们步履轻盈，让我们灵魂的褶皱不再。

Keep Walking in Sunshine
一直走在阳光里

◎ Juliet N.

Years of storms had taken their toll on the old windmill. Its wheel, rusted and fallen, lay silent in the **lush**[①] bluegrass. Its once animated silhouette was now a tall motionless steeple in the twilight sun.

I hadn't walked across our old farm in fifteen years. Yet the sensations came flooding back. I could smell the freshness of new mown alfalfa. I could feel the ping of the ice cold summer rain, and the sun's sudden warmth on my wet shoulders when it reappeared after a brisk July thunderstorm.

Rain or shine, I used to walk this path each day to see Greta. She always made me smile, even after Sis and I had just had a big **squabble**[②]. I would help Greta with her chores. Then we would visit over a generous helping of her delicious homemade chocolate cookies and ice cream. Being confined to a wheel chair didn't stop Greta from being a fabulous cook.

Greta gave me two of the greatest gifts I've ever received. First, she taught me how to read. She also taught me that when I forgave Sis for our squabbles, it meant I wouldn't keep feeling like a victim. Instead, I would feel sunny.

Mr. Dinking, the local banker, tried to foreclose on Greta's house and land

① lush [lʌʃ] adj. 苍翠繁茂的；多汁的；丰富的

② squabble ['skwɔbl] n. 争吵，口角

美丽语录

When life gives you a hundred reasons to cry, show life that you have a thousand reasons to smile.

当生活给你一百个理由哭泣时，你就拿出一千个理由笑给它看。

多年的风雨毁坏了古老的风车。它的轮子锈了，倒了，静静地躺在葱翠的早熟禾丛中。在夕阳的映衬下，曾经栩栩如生的风车如今像高耸的塔尖那般毫无生气。

我已经有 15 年没有走过我们的农场了。然而，昔日的感觉再次涌现。我仿佛闻到了刚刚修剪过的苜蓿的清新气息；感觉到了冰冷的夏雨打在我的身上；还有 7 月的雨后太阳照耀在湿漉漉的身上时那股突如其来的暖意。

无论晴天或雨天，曾经我每天都会走过这条小道去探望格丽塔。她总能逗得我开怀一笑，即使我刚和姐姐大吵了一架。我会帮助格丽塔做些家务活。接着，我们会大口大口地吃着她亲手制作的巧克力曲奇饼干和冰淇淋。即使只能靠轮椅行走，也无法阻挡格丽塔成为一个出色的厨师。

格丽塔送给我两份最好的礼物。首先，她教会了我认字。除此之外，她还教我原谅同我争吵的姐姐，让我不再觉得委屈，我的心情也跟着开朗起来。

格丽塔的丈夫去世后，当地的银行家丁肯先生试图想要收取她抵押给

after her husband passed away. Thanks to Pa and Uncle Johan, Greta got to keep everything. Pa said that it was the least he could do for someone talented enough to teach me to read!

Soon folks were coming from miles around to buy Greta's homemade cakes, pies, breads, cookies, cider, and ice cream. Hank, the grocery store man, came each week to stock his shelves and bring Greta supplies.

Greta even had me take a big apple pie to Mr. Dinking who became one of her best customers and friends. That's just how Greta was. She could turn anyone into a friend!

Greta always said, "Dear, keep walking in sunshine!"No matter how terrible my day started, I always felt sunny walking home from Greta's house—even beneath the winter starlight.

I arrived at Greta's house today just after sunset. An ambulance had stopped a few feet from her door, it's red lights flashing. When I ran into the old house, Greta recognized me right away.

She smiled at me with her unforgettable twinkling blue eyes. She was almost out of breath when she reached out and softly touched my arm. Her last words to me were "Dear, keep walking in sunshine!"

I'm sure that Greta is walking in the brightest sunshine she's ever seen. And, I'm sure that she heard every word I read at her memorial service.

I chose a beautiful verse by Leo Buscaglia. It's one that Greta taught me to read many years ago...

"Love can never grow old. Locks may lose their brown and gold. Cheeks may fade and hollow grow. But the hearts that love will know, never winter's frost and chill, summer's warmth is in them still."

银行的房子。多亏了爸爸和约翰叔叔的帮忙，格丽塔才保住了一切。爸爸说过，那是他为一位聪明得能教我识字的人做的力所能及的一件小事。

不久，方圆数英里的人们都来买格丽塔亲手做的蛋糕、馅饼、面包、曲奇饼、苹果酒和冰淇淋。杂货店的老板汉克每周都要给她送材料，并从她那儿进货。

格丽塔甚至曾经让我给丁肯先生送去一个大苹果馅饼。他也成为了她的顾客和朋友。这就是格丽塔，她可以和任何人成为朋友。

格丽塔常说："亲爱的，记得要一直走在阳光里！"无论每天一开始时有多糟糕，可是当我从格丽塔的小屋走出来之后，即使是在洒满星光的冬日，我都会觉得心情舒畅。

今天，太阳一下山，我就来到了格丽塔的家。一辆救护车正停在她家门前，车上的红灯不停地闪烁着。当我跑进那间破旧的房子时，格丽塔立刻认出了我。

她冲我微笑着，那双令人难忘的蓝眼睛闪烁着光芒。当她伸手轻轻抚摸着我的手时，她已经奄奄一息了。她对我说的最后一句话就是："亲爱的，记得要一直走在阳光里！"

我相信格丽塔此时一定漫步在她所见过的最明媚的阳光里。而且，我也相信她听见了我在她的追悼会上念的每一个字。

我选了利奥·巴斯卡格里亚的一首优美的诗歌，正是格丽塔多年前教我念的……

"爱能经久不衰。华发或许会失去原有的光彩。双颊或许会日显消瘦黯淡。然而，有爱的心中，从无寒冬霜冰，只有夏之温热。"

Advice to Youth

马克·吐温致青年人的忠告

◎ Mark Twain

Being told I would be expected to talk here, I inquired what sort of talk I ought to make. They said it should be something suitable to youth—something didactic, instructive, or something in the nature of good advice. Very well. I have a few things in my mind which I have often longed to say for the instruction of the young; for it is in one's tender early years that such things will best take root and be most enduring and most valuable, First, then. I will say to you my young friends—and I say it beseechingly, urgingly—

Always obey your parents, when they are present. This is the best policy in the long run, because if you don't, they will make you. Most parents think they know better than you do, and you can generally make more by humoring that **superstition**[①] than you can by acting on your own better judgment.

Be respectful to your superiors, if you have any, also to strangers, and sometimes to others. If a person offend you, and you are in doubt as to whether it was intentional or not, do not resort to extreme measures; simply watch your chance and hit him with a brick. That will be sufficient. If you shall find that he

① superstition [ˌsjuːpəˈstiʃə] n. 迷信；盲目崇拜；盲目恐惧

美丽语录

If you want to make your dreams come true, the first thing you have to do is wake up.

想要实现梦想，就先从梦中醒来。

听说期望我来谈谈，我便想要知道应该发表怎样的谈话。他们说应该是适合于青年人的话题，比如教育性的、启发性的，或者是一些本质上是金玉良言那类的话题。好吧！关于指导青年人，我心里其实有几件时常想要说的事。因为就是在人的幼年时期，这些事情才更容易扎根，更能持久和最有价值。那么，首先，我要对青年朋友们说的是——我诚恳地、迫切地想要说的是——

父母在场的时候，要永远服从他们。长远看来这是上策，因为如果你不服从他们的话，他们也会想方设法让你服从。大多数父母觉得他们比你懂得多，一般来说，你们相信这种迷信的说法，要比根据自以为是的判断行事来得好。

尊重你的上司，在你有了上司之后。尊重陌生人，有时也要尊重其他人。如果一个人冒犯了你，你要稍微怀疑一下，看看他们是存心的还是无心的，不要采取极端的方法。如果你发现他并无心要冒犯你，那就坦白承认自己打他是不对的。像个男子汉那样承认错误，并说声不是故意的。是的，永远都不要采用暴力。身在这个充满仁慈善意的时代里，暴力的时代

had not intended any offense, come out frankly and confess yourself in the wrong when you struck him; acknowledge it like a man and say you didn't mean to. Yes, always avoid violence; in this age of charity and kindliness, the time has gone by for such things. Leave dynamite to the low and **unrefined**①.

Go to bed early, get up early—this is wise. Some authorities say get up with the sun; some say get up with one thing, others with another. But a lark is really the best thing to get up with. It gives you a splendid reputation with everybody to know that you get up with the lark; and if you get the right kind of lark, and work at him right, you can easily train him to get up at half past nine, every time—it's no trick at all.

Now as to the matter of lying, you want to be very careful about lying; otherwise you are nearly sure to get caught. Once caught, you can never again be in the eyes to the good and the pure, what you were before. Many a young person has injured himself permanently through a single clumsy and ill finished lie, the result of carelessness born of incomplete training. Some authorities hold that the young out not to lie at all. That of course, is putting it rather stronger than necessary; still while I cannot go quite so far as that, I do maintain, and I believe I am right, that the young ought to be temperate in the use of this great art until practice and experience shall give them that confidence, elegance, and precision which alone can make the accomplishment graceful and profitable. Patience, diligence, painstaking attention to detail—these are requirements; these in time, will make the student perfect; upon these only, may he rely as the sure foundation for future eminence. Think what tedious years of study, thought, practice, experience, went to the equipment of that peerless old master who was

① unrefined ['ʌnri'faind] adj. 未提炼的；不高尚的；粗俗的

已然远去。把“炸药”留给低俗又无教养的人吧！

早睡早起——这是一种明智之举。有些权威人士说要跟着太阳起床；而有些则说跟着这个东西起床，其他人说跟着那个东西起床。然而，跟着云雀起床是最好不过了。你因此获得好名声，人人都知道你跟着云雀起床。如果你有幸找到一只好的云雀，在它身上花点功夫，你能很容易地把它训练成每天九点半起床——这可不是骗人的把戏。

现在来谈谈说谎的问题。你要小心应付说谎，否则你被揭穿的机会十有八九。一旦被揭穿，在善良和纯洁的目光中，你再也不是以前的你了。许多青年人，由于接受的教育不完整而导致处事轻率，从而编造了一个难以自圆其说的笨拙谎言，最后伤害了自己。一些权威人士认为青年人根本不该说谎。当然，这种说法有点过于偏激，或者说情况并非真的如此。虽然我无法把话说得太过，但我仍然坚信自己的观点是正确的。我认为青年人应该适当地运用这门伟大的艺术，当然前提条件是他们从实践和经验身上获得了信心、高雅和严谨。因为这三点中的任何一点都能让谎言变得高雅、有益。耐心、勤奋和细致入微——这些都是必要的素质。随着时间的推移，这些素质能够让学生变得完美。有了这些，只要有了这些，他才能为以后的功成名就打下坚实的基础。试想一下，通过多年乏味的学习、思考、实践、亲身体验，那位盖世无双的大师才能拥有这些素质，才能强迫整个世界接受“真理是强大的，而且终将取得胜利！”这句崇高而掷地有声的格言——这句关于事实的复杂层面说出的最崇高的话，任何一个女人都未曾获得过。因为人类的历史和每个个人的经验都深深地将这样的证据埋藏起来：一个真理不难抹杀，可一个巧妙的谎言却能经久不衰。波士顿有个纪念碑，专门为发现麻醉法的人而立的。后来人们才知道，那个人根本就没有发现麻醉法，他只是盗取了另一个人的发现。

这个真理强大吗？它能最终取得胜利吗？唉，不会的。听众们，纪念

able to impose upon the whole world the lofty and sounding maxim that "Truth is mighty and will prevail"— the most **majestic**[①] compound fracture of fact which any of woman born has yet achieved. For the history of our race, and each individual's experience, are sewn thick with evidences that a truth is not hard to kill, and that a lie well told is immortal. There is in Boston a monument of the man who discovered anesthesia; many people are aware, in these latter days, that that man didn't discover it at all, but stole the discovery from another man.

Is this truth mighty, and will it prevail? Ah no, my hearers, the monument is made of hardy material, but the lie it tells will outlast it a million years. An awkward, feeble, leaky lie is a thing which you ought to make it your unceasing study to avoid; such a lie as that has no more real permanence than an average truth. Why, you might as well tell the truth at once and be done with it. A feeble, stupid, preposterous lie will not live two years—except it be a slander upon somebody. It is indestructible, then of course, but that is no merit of yours. A final word: begin your practice of this gracious and beautiful art early—begin now. If I had begun earlier, I could have learned how.

① majestic [mə'dʒestik] adj. 雄伟的，威严的，崇高的

碑是用坚硬的材料建成的，但它向世人说的谎却比它持久百万年。一个笨拙的、不攻自破的、漏洞百出的谎言是你应该不断学会避免的东西。这样的谎言甚至不比一个普通的事实来得更具真实的永恒性。那你为何不既讲真话又相信真理呢？一个不攻自破的、愚蠢的、荒谬的谎言持续不了两年——除非是对某人的诽谤。因为那种谎言是牢不可破的，当然那也不是你值得夸耀的东西。最后说一句：早点开始实践这门高雅美妙的艺术——立刻开始吧！如果我能早点开始实践，我想我已经学会这门艺术了。

Walking Tours
徒步旅行

◎ Robert Louis Stevenson

It must not be imagined that a walking tour, as some would have us fancy, is merely a better or worse way of seeing the country. There are many ways of seeing landscape quite as good; and none more vivid, in spite of canting **dilettantes**[①], than from a railway train. But landscape on a walking tour is quite accessory. He who is indeed of the brotherhood does not voyage inquest of the picturesque, but of certain jolly humors of the hope and spirit with which the march begins at morning, and the peace and spiritual repletion of the evening's rest. He cannot tell whether he puts his knapsack on, or takes it off, with more delight. The excitement of the **departure**[②] puts him in key for that of the arrival. Whatever he does is not only a reward in itself, but will be further rewarded in the sequel; and so pleasure leads on to pleasure in an endless chain. It is this that so few can understand; they will either be always lounging or always at five miles an hour; they do not play off the one against the other, prepare allay for the evening, and all evening for the next day. And, above all, it is here that

① dilettante [ˌdiliˈtænti] n.（艺术等的）一知半解者；业余爱好者

② departure [diˈpɑːtʃə] n. 离开；出发，起程；违背，变更

美丽语录

I am a slow walker, but I never walk backwards.

虽然我走得很慢，但是我从来不后退。

无法想象一些人只是把徒步旅行看成是一种观赏乡村风景的还行或糟糕的方式。其实观赏山水风景的方式很多，而且都还不错，只是没有一种比坐火车观赏来得生动有趣——只有那些附庸风雅的人不赞同这个观点。但是，徒步观赏山水美景真的是一个不错的选择。一个真正懂得兄弟情怀的人乘船出游时，他所追求的并非是沿途秀丽的风光，而是一种欢愉之情——从清晨满怀希望、精神抖擞地出航，到夜晚平安、充实地归航。他说不出是背上行囊时更快乐，还是卸下行囊时更快乐。出航时的兴奋预示了他归航时的喜悦。无论他做了什么，都不仅仅是对其本身的奖赏，也将在接下来的日子里获得更丰厚的奖赏。所以，快乐带来快乐，源源不断。但是，只有少数的人明白这一点。大多数的人们不是原地不动，就是顷刻数里。他们不懂得如何将这两者折中，只知道昼夜不分地忙碌着。最重要的是，赶路人无法体会旅行带来的乐趣。他只许自己举杯畅饮，却看不得别人小酌一杯。他不相信，小酌才能品出真正的酒香。他不会相信，拼命赶路只会让自己变得呆板、冷酷。晚上回到旅馆，只会感觉疲惫不堪、昏

your overwalker fails of comprehension. His heart rises against those who drink their curacaos in liqueur glasses, when he himself can swill it in a brown John. He will not believe that the flavor is more delicate in the smaller dose. He will not believe that to walk this unconscionable distance is merely to stupefy and brutalize himself, and come to his inn, at night, with a sort of frost on his five wits, and a starless night of darkness in his spirit. Not for him the mild luminous evening of the temperate walker! He has nothing left of man but a physical need for bed-time and a double nightcap; and even his pipe, if he be a smoker, will be savorless and disenchanted. It is the fate of such a one to take twice as much trouble as is needed to obtain happiness, and miss the happiness in the end; he is the man of the proverb, in short, who goes farther and fares worse.

Now, to be properly enjoyed, a walking tour should beg one upon alone. If you go in a company, or even in pairs, it is no longer a walking tour in anything but name; it is something else and more in the nature of a picnic. A walking tour should be gone upon alone, because freedom is of the essence; because you should be able to stop and go on, and follow this way or that, as the freak takes you; and because you must have your own pace, and neither trot alongside a champion walker, nor mince in time with a girl. And then you must be open to all impressions and let your thoughts take color from what you see. You should be as a pipe for any wind to play upon. "I cannot see the wit," says Hazlitt, "of walking and talking at the same time. When I am in the country I wish to vegetate like the country," which is the gist of all that can be said upon the matter. There should be no cackle of voices at your elbow, to jar on the meditative silence of the morning. And so long as a man is reasoning he cannot surrender himself to

昏沉沉。夜晚对他来说，并不像悠闲的漫步者眼中那样温和醉人。他唯一的需求就是睡帽和上床睡觉。如果他是一个吸烟的人，甚至就连他的烟斗也会变得索然无味，没有任何吸引力。这种人注定会在追求幸福的过程中事倍功半，而且，他最终还是和幸福擦肩而过了。总之，他就如同谚语里所说的那种人——走得越远越糟糕。

现在，好好地享受旅行吧！徒步旅行者必须力求独自前行。如果结伴而行抑或成双成对，那就不再是徒步旅行了，只是徒有虚名罢了；它就更像是在大自然中举行的一场野餐。徒步旅行者必须力求独自前行，因为自由就是独自徒步旅行的；因为你能随时停下或继续前进，随心所欲地选择这条路或那条路；因为你必须要有自己的步调，既不需要跟随拼命赶路的人，也不需要在一个女孩身上浪费时间。然而，你必须敞开心扉接受所有的情感，让你所见到的东西为思想添彩。你应该做一支随风飘零的笛子。哈兹里特曾经这样说道："我无法体会行走和谈论同时进行的乐趣。当我身在乡村时，我渴望过着简单淳朴的乡村生活。"这就是徒步旅行的真正涵义了。你身边不该有类似咯咯叫的嘈杂声，打破了清晨冥想时的宁静。只要一个人无法停止思考，那他就无法全身心陶醉在户外的美景中。陶醉始于意乱眼迷、思维停滞，并最终进入一种超凡的平和境界。

任何形式的旅行，第一天总会有些酸楚的瞬间。当旅行者厌倦了自己的行囊，甚至想要把它扔到篱笆外时，他就会像基督徒处于类似情况那样，

that fine **intoxication**[①] that comes of much motion in the open air, that begins in a sort of dazzle and sluggishness of the brain, and ends in a peace that passes comprehension.

During the first day or so of any tour there are moments of bitterness, when the traveler feels more than coldly towards his knapsack, when he is half in a mind to throw it bodily over the hedge and, like Christian on a similar occasion, "give three leaps and go on singing". And yet it soon acquires a property of easiness. It becomes magnetic; the spirit of the journey enters into it. And no sooner have you passed the straps over your shoulder than the lees of sleep are cleared from you, you pull yourself together with a shake, and fall at once into your stride. And surely, of all possible moods, this, in which a man takes the road, is the best. Of course, if he will keep thinking of his anxieties, if he will open the merchant Abudah's chest and walk arm-in-arm with the hag—why, wherever he is, and whether he walks fast or slow, the chances are that he will not be happy. And so much the more shame to himself! There are perhaps thirty men setting forth at that same hour, and I would lay a large wager there is not another dull face among the thirty. It would be a fine thing to follow, in a coat of darkness, one after another of these wayfarers, some summer morning, for the first few miles upon the road. This one, who walks fast, with a keen look in his eyes, is all concentrated in his own mind; he is up at his loom, weaving and weaving, to set the landscape to words. This one peers about, as he goes, among the grasses; he waits by the canal to watch the dragonflies; he leans on the gate of the pasture, and cannot look enough upon the complacent kine. And here comes another, talking, laughing, and gesticulating to himself. His face changes from time to

① intoxication [in,tɔksi'keiʃən] n. 醉；陶醉；极度兴奋

“跳三跳，接着唱”。不过，你很快就能获得出游时的舒适感。它会变得十分有吸引力；出游时的那份精神也会与其融合在一起。于是，当你将行囊背在肩上时，你残留的睡意瞬间消失不见，你将精神抖擞地大踏步开始自己的新旅行。当然，在所有心情中，选择道路时的心情是最好的。当然，如果他继续思考着自己的烦心事，如果他像阿布达的箱子那样敞开着跟随女巫同行，那么，无论他身在哪里，不论他是匆匆赶路还是悠闲漫步，他都不会快乐的。而且，这让他的人生蒙羞。如果现在有 30 个人同时出发，我敢保证，在这 30 人当中，你再也看不到一张忧郁的脸。这是一件值得去做的事情。试想一下，一个夏日的清晨，这些徒步旅行者披着夜色，一个接一个地上路了。他们当中有个步调很快的人，他的眼中充满渴望，全神贯注于自己的思绪，原来他正在自出机杼，斟字酌句，把山水美景写成文字。有一个人一边走一边眯着眼睛看着草丛；他在小河边停下了，他想要看看飞舞的蜻蜓；他倾着身子靠在牧场的门边，看不够那怡然自得的老黄牛。另一个人则说着，笑着，冲着自己手舞足蹈。他的脸色随着眼中闪现的怒火或是额头上出现的阴云而不断地变化着。他正在路边构思文章，发表演说，进行最富激情的面谈。他很有可能过一会就开始高歌一曲了。

对他而言，假使他并不擅长这门艺术，又碰巧在拐角处碰见一个感觉

time, as indignation flashes from his eyes or anger clouds his forehead. He is composing articles, delivering orations, and conducting the most impassioned interviews, by the way. A little farther on, and it is as like as not he will begin to sing.

And well for him, supposing him to be no great master in that art, if he stumbles across no stolid peasant at a corner; for on such an occasion, I scarcely know which is the more troubled, or whether it is worse to suffer the confusion of your **troubadour**①, or the unfeigned alarm of your clown. A sedentary population, accustomed, besides, to the strange mechanical bearing of the common tramp, can in no wise explain to itself the gaiety of these passers-by. I knew one man who was arrested as a runaway lunatic, because although a full-grown person with a red beard, he skipped as he went like a child. And you would be astonished if I were to tell you all the grave and learned heads who have confessed to me that, when on walking tours, they sang—and sang very ill—and had a pair of red ears when, as described above, the inauspicious peasant plumped into their arms from round a corner.

① troubadour ['tru:bəduə] n. 吟游诗人

并不迟钝的农民，我想不出还有什么是比这样的情形来得糟糕，我不知道是这位年轻的民谣歌手更尴尬，还是那位农民更难受。还有一类人，他们久居室内，而且不喜欢去陌生的地方，所以这些人也无法体会旅行者的快乐。我认识一个人，他曾经被当作疯汉抓起来，只因为他看上去像个蓄着红胡子的成年人，走路却像小孩那样蹦蹦跳跳。当我告诉你下面这些事时，你肯定会很吃惊，那就是：很多学识渊博的人向我坦白，他们徒步旅行时也会唱歌，而且唱得十分难听，当他们遇到上面提到的情形——和一个倒霉的农民在拐角相遇时，他们也会羞愧难当。

Finding What You Do Not Seek

探寻未知的美好

◎ Orison Marden

Dining one day with Baron James Rothschild, Eugene Delacroix, the famous French artist, confessed that, during some time past, he had vainly sought for a head to serve as a model for that of a beggar in a picture which he was painting; and that, as he gazed at his host's features, the idea suddenly occurred to him that the very head he desired was before him. Rothschild, being a great lover of art, readily consented to sit as the beggar. The next day, at the studio, Delacroix placed a tunic around the baron's shoulders, put a stout staff in his hand, and made him pose as if he were resting on the steps of an ancient Roman temple. In this attitude he was found by one of the artist's favorite pupils, in a brief absence of the master from the room. The youth naturally concluded that the beggar had just been brought in, and with a **sympathetic**① look quietly slipped a piece of money into his hand. Rothschild thanked him simply, pocketed the money, and the student passed out. Rothschild then inquired of the master, and found that the young man had talent, but very slender means.

Soon after, the youth received a letter stating that charity bears interest, and

① sympathetic [,simpə'θetik] adj. 有同情心的；赞同的，支持的；和谐的

美丽语录

If you want a happy life, tie it to a goal, not to people or things.

如果你想过得快乐，把生活跟目标联系在一起，而不是跟某个人或某些事。

一天，在詹姆士·罗斯柴尔德爵士家的宴会上，法国著名艺术家欧仁·德拉克洛瓦当场向我袒露心声：在过去的一段时间里，他一直苦苦地为自己正在创作的画作找寻一位乞丐模特。当他的目光停在爵士的身上时，脑中突然闪现一个灵感——他梦寐以求的模特就在眼前。作为一个狂热的艺术爱好者，罗斯柴尔德欣然答应了扮演一名乞丐模特。第二天，在画室里，德拉克洛瓦拿了一件束腰外套披在爵士的肩上，让爵士手拿一根短棍，并摆出一个造型，就像是正在一座古罗马神庙前的阶梯上休息一样。接着，德拉克洛瓦便离开了画室一小会儿。这时，他最得意的一名学生进来看到了爵士的乞丐造型。这位年轻人自然而然地认为这个乞丐是刚来到画室的，于是，他显现出充满同情的表情，一声不响地把一些钱塞进他的手里。罗斯柴尔德只是轻轻地道了一声谢谢，就把钱放进兜里。那个学生走出了画室。后来，罗斯柴尔德从画家那儿得知，这个年轻人其实很有绘画天赋，但就是缺少处世经验。

不久，那个年轻人就收到了一封信，信的内容大概是这样的：由于他

that the accumulated interest on the amount he had given to one he supposed to be a beggar was represented by the sum of ten thousand francs, which was awaiting his claim at the Rothschild office.

This illustrates well the art to cheerful amusement even if one has great business cares—the entertainment of the artist, the personation of a beggar, and an act of beneficence toward a worthy student.

It was said by Wilhelm von Humboldt, that "it is worthy of special remark that when we are not too anxious about happiness and unhappiness, but devote ourselves to the strict and unsparing performance of duty, then happiness comes of itself."

Are not buoyant spirits like water sparkling when it runs? "I have found my greatest happiness in labor," said Gladstone. "I early formed a habit of industry, and it has been its own reward. The young are apt to think that rest means a cessation from all effort, but I have found the most perfect rest in changing effort. If brain-weary over books and study, go out into the blessed sunlight and the pure air, and give heartfelt exercise to the body. The brain will soon become calm and rested. The efforts of Nature are **ceaseless**[①]. Even in our sleep the heart throbs on. I try to live close to Nature, and to imitate her in my labors. The compensation is sound sleep, a wholesome digestion, and powers that are kept at their best; and this, I take it, is the chief reward of industry."

Those only are happy who have their minds fixed on some object other than their own happiness. "The most delicate, the most sensible of all pleasures," says La Bruyre, "consists in promoting the pleasures of others."

And Hawthorne has said that the inward pleasure of imparting pleasure is

① ceaseless ['si:slis] adj. 不停的，不间断的

的善良本性，把钱给了一个他认为是乞丐的人。为此，他将得到一万法郎的奖赏，他可以随时到罗斯柴尔德的办公室领取。

这件事充分说明了艺术有着令人愉快的魅力，即使是富人也不另外——画家的灵感、假扮的乞丐和可敬的学生的善意之举。

威廉·冯·洪堡曾经说过："当我们不再为是否快乐而忧心，而是全心全意地严格履行自己的职责时，快乐自然就会来临。"

快乐的感觉不就像是水光荡漾的河水吗？格拉德斯顿曾经说过："劳作给了我最大的快乐。我从小就养成了勤奋的习惯，并因此受益匪浅。年轻人总是觉得休息就意味着停止一切努力，但我认为最好的休息就是转变成为另一种努力。如果过重的学习压力使你头昏脑胀，那就出去晒一些温暖的阳光，呼吸一下新鲜的空气，好好放松放松身心。那样的话，大脑就能很快恢复平静并得到充足的休息。天性的努力是永无休止的，即使睡觉时，我们的心脏也会不停地跳动着。我试着让自己的生活顺应天性，并在劳动中尽力模仿。于是，我得到了：舒适的睡眠、健康的消化能力和旺盛的精力。而我所得到的这些都是勤奋的主要回报。"

只有那些把精力集中在某个目标上，而不是执著于个人幸福的人，才能获得真正的快乐。拉·布鲁耶尔曾经说过："最美妙、最明智的快乐是和他人共同分享快乐。"

霍桑也曾经说过，与人分享的快乐才是最顶级的快乐。

从前有个国王，他十分宠爱自己的小儿子，他想尽办法让小儿子开心。因此，国王买来小马给小儿子骑；建造漂亮的房间给他住；还有图画、书本、数不清的玩具、给他上课的老师、玩伴和其他一切可以用钱能做得到的事情。可这一切都无法让小王子感到快乐。无论走到哪，他总是一副愁眉苦脸的样子，他总想着得到自己没有的东西。直到一位魔术师来到宫里，这一切才有所改变。魔术师看到愁眉苦脸的小男孩后，他对国王说道："我

the choicest of all.

There was once a king who loved his little boy very much, and took a great deal of pains to please him. So he gave him a pony to ride, beautiful rooms to live in, pictures, books, toys without number, teachers, companions, and everything that money could buy or ingenuity devise; but for all this, the young prince was unhappy. He wore a frown wherever he went, and was always wishing for something he did not have. At length a magician came to the court. He saw the scowl on the boy's face, and said to the king: "I can make your son happy, and turn his frowns into smiles, but you must pay me a great price for telling him this secret."

"All right," said the king, "whatever you ask I will give." The magician took the boy into a private room. He wrote something with a white substance on a piece of paper. He gave the boy a candle, and told him to light it and hold it under the paper, and then see what he could read. Then the magician went away. The boy did as he had been told, and the white letters turned into a beautiful blue. They formed these words: "Do a kindness to some one every day." The prince followed the advice, and became the happiest boy in the realm.

Happy is he who has no sense of discord with the harmony of the universe, who is open to the voices of nature and of the spiritual realm, and who sees the light that never was on sea or land. Such a life can but give expression to its inward harmony. Every pure and healthy thought, every noble aspiration for the good and the true, every longing of the heart for a higher and better life, every lofty purpose and unselfish endeavor, makes the human spirit stronger, more harmonious, and more beautiful.

能让您的儿子快乐起来，将他的苦脸变成笑脸。但你必须用大笔的钱向我买下这个秘密。”

“好吧，”国王答道，“不管你要什么，我都会答应的。”于是，魔术师把小男孩带到一个单独的房间里。他用一个白色的东西在一张纸上写了些东西。然后，他递给小男孩一根蜡烛，并叫他把这张纸点燃后，再放到蜡烛的上方，看看能读到什么东西。说完这些话，魔术师就离开了房间。小男孩照他说的话做了，只见白色的字母变成了美丽的蓝色，并组成了一句话：“每天为他人做一件好事。”小王子接受了这个建议，成了王国里最快乐的人。

真正快乐的人，他丝毫不会觉得自己和宇宙之间是不和谐的；他会敞开心扉倾听来自天性和精神世界里的声音；他能看见天地间从未展现过的光芒。只有这样的生命才能表达出内心的和谐。每一个纯洁健康的思想，每一种对善良和真理的崇高向往，每一颗渴望更高尚、更美好生活的心，每一个崇高的目标和每一次无私的努力，都让人类的精神变得更坚强、更和谐、更美好。

Go Easy and Enjoy Yourself in Harmony
飘逸而行

◎ Karen Rohlf

To go on a journey is often **worrisome**[①], but so long as one lives he proceeds on his life's journey. Different people go along differently. Some take hasty steps in anxiety. Obsessed with reaching the next goal in time, they spare no time for sight-seeing along the way, nor do they have a clear view where their long roads end. Others travel **leisurely**[②] like tourists. They would take time off now and then for a look at blooming flowers or fallen petals. They would stop to admire clouds gathering and dispersing. Even when they go against the wind or are caught in the rain, they never get annoyed, for worries slip off their minds as if from an open net.

Cramped is one's workplace. Narrow is one's residence and small is the social circle one moves about—such limitedness in space entail lack of variety which is the source of some people's complaint. But a person is always able to find space and comfort if he takes things as they are... Compared with the nastness of the universe it is only a tiny spot one occupies on earth. However,

① worrisome ['wʌrisəm] adj. 令人烦恼的；闷闷不乐的

② leisurely ['li:ʒəli] adv. 从容不迫地，慢慢地

丽语录

The simple diet can protect the stomach; the fresh air can wash the lung. We should enjoy the sunshine, spend more time with friends and forget the tiredness in the world.

用粗茶淡饭养胃，用清新空气洗肺，让灿烂阳光晒背，得空和朋友聚聚会，忘却辗转尘世的累。

人在旅途，不安和困惑在所难免，但只要你活着，你就要继续你的人生之旅。不同的人有着不同的行进方式。有些人步履匆忙，焦虑不安，只盼着能及时完成下一个目标，他们根本无暇观赏路边的风景，也不知道茫茫路途何处是终点。另一些人则像旅游那般不紧不慢，时而停下赏花谢花开，看云卷云舒；时而逆风而行，在雨中前行，他们从不苦恼，因为忧虑已从敞开的心网中被过滤掉了。

狭小的办公场所，拥窄的居住空间，局限的社交圈——人们对这些一成不变的“有限”感到不满。然而，如果一个人随遇而安，总能找到安宁与舒适。浩瀚的大千世界，一个人只能占据其中微小的一个位置。可比海洋更宽广的是天空，比天空更宽广的是人的胸怀，因为小小心灵有一对想象的翅膀，它可以尽情翱翔。

though larger than the ocean is the sky, even larger is the human mind, for in it imagination would come and go on the wing without limitations.

One may eventually win what he has set his mind to, only to find that he has lost quite a lot. Perhaps what he loses is even better than what he gains.

On one's journey of life some people hurry on with a heavy heart in pursuit of fame and wealth while others go easy and enjoy themselves in harmony with nature.

只有当一个人发觉自己失去了许多时，他才能最终得到他想要的东西，不过也有可能是得不偿失。

人生旅途上，一些人带着重重的追求名利之心前行，而另一些人则逍遥自在地和大自然和谐相处，飘逸而行。

How to Stay Young
让青春常驻

◎ Harvey Bingham

Throw out **nonessential**[1] numbers. This includes age, weight and height. Let the doctor worry about them. That's why you pay him/her.

Keep only cheerful friends. The grouches pull you down.

Keep learning. Learn more about the computer, crafts, gardening, whatever. Never let the brain idle. "An **idle**[2] mind is the devil's workshop. And the devil's name is Alzheimer's."

Enjoy the simple things.

Laugh often, long and loud. Laugh until you gasp for breath.

The tears happen. Endure, grieve, and move on. The only person who is with us our entire life, is ourselves. Be alive while you are alive.

Surround yourself with what you love, whether it's family, pets, keepsakes, music, plants, hobbies, whatever. Your home is your **refuge**[3].

Cherish your health: If it is good, preserve it. If it is unstable, improve it. If it is beyond what you can improve, get help.

---

① nonessential [ˌnɔniˈsenʃəl] adj. 非本质的；不重要的

② idle [ˈaidl] adj. 空闲的；懒惰的；无所事事的

③ refuge [ˈrefjuːdʒ] n. 躲避；避难所，藏身处

美丽语录

Remember these simple guidelines for happiness: 1. Free your heart from hate; 2. Free your mind from worry; 3. Live simply; 4. Give more; 5. Expect less.

幸福五大原则：1. 心中无恨；2. 脑中无忧；3. 生活简单；4. 多些付出；5. 少些期待。

扔掉那些无关紧要的数字。包括你的年龄、体重和身高。让医生去操心吧。因为你给了他们报酬。

结交乐观的朋友。那些满腹牢骚的人只能让你雪上加霜。

学无止境。多了解计算机、手艺、园艺等知识。不要让你的大脑闲置下来。“无所事事的大脑是魔鬼的加工厂。魔鬼的名字叫痴呆症。”

享受简单事物。

多笑，开怀大笑。上气不接下气地笑。

有泪就流。忍受和悲伤过后，要继续前行。陪伴我们度过一生的惟一的人——就是我们自己。让生命鲜活起来。

让你的所爱环绕着你，无论是家人、宠物、纪念品、音乐、植物、爱好，什么都好。你的家就是你的避风港。

珍惜健康：如果它很好，就好好地保护它。如果它反复无常，就改善它。如果你已无力改善它了，就请别人帮忙吧。

别踏上犯罪的道路。你可以去商场闲逛，可以去邻县游荡，可以出国旅行，但不要踏上犯罪之路。

Don't take guilt trips. Take a trip to the mall, to the next country, to a foreign country, but not to where the guilt is.

Tell the people you love that you love them, at every opportunity.

And always remember: Life is not measured by the number of breaths we take, but by the moments that take our breath away.

告诉你所爱的人们，你爱他们，把握每一个表达的机会。

永远记住：度量生命的不是我们呼吸的次数，而是那些最最难忘的时刻。

If you want something,

don't wish for it. Life is too short to wait.

如果你想要某样东西，

别等着有人会送给你。生命太短，等不得。